A TOUCH OF FLAME

This book brings together more than 100 poems
by contemporary Christian poets. Some are well
known. Many are little known. All deserve wider
recognition.

The selection is not confined to 'religious'
poems. Its broad themes offer a rich variety:
nativity, incarnation, commonplace, laughter
and tears, landscape, beatitude, way of the cross,
resurrection . . . And the poems themselves both
touch and delight the reader. They restore to a
hungry world the lost dimension of wonder.

JENNY ROBERTSON is herself a poet and
writer, the author of children's novels, and a
playwright. She lives in Edinburgh.

A TOUCH
OF
FLAME

An anthology of contemporary Christian poetry

Compiled by
JENNY ROBERTSON

*For Lizzy
With much love on
your birthday.
Debbie xx
16th June 1989.*

A LION PAPERBACK
Oxford · Batavia · Sydney

This collection © 1989 Jenny Robertson
All poems are copyright and appear by permission of the authors
For works previously published, see Acknowledgments on p. 183

Published by
Lion Publishing plc
Sandy Lane West, Littlemore, Oxford, England
ISBN 0 7459 1509 4
Lion Publishing Corporation
1705 Hubbard Avenue, Batavia, Illinois 60510, USA
ISBN 0 7459 1509 4
Albatross Books Pty Ltd
PO Box 320, Sutherland, NSW 2232, Australia
ISBN 0 7324 0045 7

First edition 1989

British Library Cataloguing-in-Publication Data

A Touch of flame : an anthology of
contemporary Christian poetry.
1. Christian poetry in English, 1945– .
Anthologies
I. Robertson, Jenny
821′.914′080382

ISBN 0–7459–1509–4

Library of Congress Cataloging-in-Publication Data

A Touch of flame : an anthology of contemporary Christian poetry/
compiled by Jenny Robertson—1st ed.
p.   cm.
A Lion paperback
ISBN 0–7459–1509–4
1. Christian poetry, English   2. English poetry—20th century.
I. Robertson, Jenny.
PR1195.C48T68 1989
821′.91′080382—dc 19

Printed in Great Britain
by Cox and Wyman, Reading

CONTENTS

COMMONPLACE

LAUGHTER AND TEARS

LANDSCAPE

BEATITUDE

WAY OF THE CROSS

RESURRECTION

A TOUCH OF FLAME

INTRODUCTION

Poetry has always been part of the fabric of my life, just like hot cross buns, Christmas, friendships or the sight of bare trees across a sunset sky. So when I started to put this anthology together, I wanted to find work which would appeal to everyone: fun poems, poems which read well aloud, poems which explore the heights and the depths of our common pilgrimage. I want readers who are unfamiliar with poetry to feel at home here. I should like those who have been 'put off' to experience the meeting-place which poetry offers, and discover that poetry as always brings its own 'touch of flame'. As we encounter a poem we find, as one of the poems here so well expresses it, the 'love-knot' at the heart of things, the 'harmony that centres all' (Jennifer Dines, *The Icon*).

Many, many people, old and young, from many walks of life sent me their poems, as the biographies given here show. Poetry *is* for everyone, but poetry is not just a spontaneous out-pouring of words. It is a craft. A poet is a wordsmith who structures the raw material of experience into something as tangible as a piece of pottery, or a new-made loaf; something as mysterious as a melody. I looked for that, too, when I chose poems, and I make no apology that some of the work here will require rather more effort on the part of the reader, work which will be richly rewarded. After all, it is the crustiest bread which is most worth eating.

Always I looked for poems, not for inspirational verse, but because I was putting together an anthology of Christian poetry I looked for poems which were written by minds attuned to Christian thought, and I worked within the framework of the Good News, the Gospel, so that the poems here, like the story of the Word made flesh, set within a physical landscape, take us through birth, love, laughter, pain and death to reawakening, resurrection, wonder.

The poems in this anthology, joyful or sorrowful, exalted or delighting in the everyday, are warp and weft of a fabric 'ancient and ragged as Adam's wearing', the very garb of all humanity which the Incarnate Word weaves into a seamless robe of wonder.

JENNY ROBERTSON

NATIVITY

AUBADE

Already the sun has outdated darkness, another morning
Pacemakes history, man the word-bearer reawakes
And dares to praise. Begging for my tongue of fire

I proclaim the motto theme, naming in ecstasy
The mystery of time. Always I crave the centre —
Serenity suffused by passion, inexhaustible yet complete.

Although I celebrate, I still hear the metronome's
Remorseless beat. No rubato here, no facile emancipation;
Accomplices in the scheme, each day encapsulates our biography.

It is January. Secretly a season turns in panegyric rondo,
A rhythm clueing us in, we sense the flicker of incarnation;
Time and timelessness interweave, countersubjects in this fugue.

MICHEAL O'SIADHAIL

FIRST SNOWS

The first feathers of the snow
Fall among swans, all year
They have guarded such whiteness for themselves;
Now, on iron water, among stone
Arches of branches, amid cold,
In the grey tent of winter
Are the snowbirds reborn.

Early flakes, fine as drizzle.
Tease the pewter mask of river,
Night frost has cracked the reed, enamelled bracken;
And the hard white, remaining late,
Fills as snow sails
Unfold through all the fields,
Bear the winter ship.

MARTYN HALSALL

CHRISTMAS CARD

Never before do I remember
    snow in November,
garlanding trees with a glory out of time;
    and the rime
sparkling in a full moon's sight —
    beauty beyond delight.
Then the Christ-month coming after
    bringing with laughter
    fog, mist and rain.

    And once again
we offer the cheerful platitudes — robins and holly.
    such folly,
when Christ came so stilly to be born
    here on that morn.

MYRA REEVES

THE CHRISTMAS CARDS

Still it persists, the myth of snow at Christmas,
Unashamedly across all our cards;
Not a few flakes but deep drifts —
Villages cosily half buried in it,
Trees, it would seem, gladly bearing its weight,
Edwardian women wrapped in furs and skating,
Santa Claus showing us the story of the Father
For ever offering the marvellous unattainable gift,
Piercing a way through darkness to the hearth.

The Nativity may be ignored but new life is hoped for.
About this the cheap cards are surely right.
For white is everybody's secret emblem:
We half perceive the meaning of the virgin snow.

SISTER MARY LAURENCE

CHRISTMAS POEM

We are folded all
In a green fable
And we fare
From early
Plough-and-daffodil sun
Through a revel
Of wind-tossed oats and barley,
Past sickle and flail
To harvest home,
The circles of bread and ale
At the long table.
It is told, the story,
We and earth and sun and corn are one.

Now kings and shepherds have come.
A winter hovel
Hides a glory
Whiter than snowflake or silver or star.

GEORGE MACKAY BROWN

DESERT ROSE

No one will sing your beauty, the poet said —
You must live and die alone.

Three travellers out of the morning rode.
They lingered.
They stirred my incense. They journeyed on.

No shower or shade —
I suffered all day the barren gold of the sun.

A star lifted its head
And seemed to murmur to me alone.

All beyond time are made,
star and poem, cornstalk and stone.

Now to the House-of-Bread
I guide three hungry gold-burdened men.

Midnight, rejoicing, shed
Dew in my cup like wine.

GEORGE MACKAY BROWN

CANDLES

Where they put, after fires,
stone upon stone again with skill and hope,
the candles shone in the cathedral
before Mary and her blessed babe.
There was a night when mother and child were caught
in the light of candles that fell from heaven:
an extension of political will.

Candle of the sky, candle of the altar,
easy for the same hand to light them.

The altar candle is lit by guilt and hope;
it is a monstrous righteousness that throws
down from the neutrality of the skies
the great candles of death.

WILLIAM NEILL
The author's translation from his own original Gaelic

PEACE

The light sings to itself in sheer content
And darkness cannot touch it. Everywhere
A thousand specks of human brightness stud
And speckle darkness' thick black soil like grain.
Voices buzz round in the next room, yet peace
Like a still sea washes against my soul.
The blaze that boils within the flesh dies down,
And I can almost sense the stubble fields.
Free of the burden of the busy wheat,
Sipping the rain that softens the dry spikes
Of hard persistent soil. The wind walks round
The trees, counting each one, gently lifts off
The leaves, lays them down to rest in earth. The streams
Flow down the channel of the dark, and paths
Lean forward to their goal, while the hills draw
Soft cloudy blankets round themselves and sleep.

Why am I drawn to twilight and the dark,
More than the summer's bitter, blazing day?
Perhaps because the Christ was born at night,
Because the year,
The gasping, panting heat now laid to rest,
Slopes gently down
Towards a cradle, and is born below
The snowflakes of the stars. The winds now guide
The hesitating days on to their aim,
And now the world and day fall back, and leave
My soul clear and complete within this span
Of silence. Anger, ache will come again,
And yet each night when drops of calm descend
Will open out a room within my heart
Where God can talk,
Fashion a peace, and find my soul once more.

RAYNE MACKINNON
This poem won second prize in the Sri Chin Moy (USA) Peace Competition

THE WARBETH BROTHERS AT CHRISTMAS

1

We have wandered, unfaithful
Even at ploughtime
Leaving the ox in the half-made furrow.

And in the time of green shoots
We turned away
From the black wings, from worm in the root.

We presumed
To sit and eat with harvesters at lowsing-time.

Now, in the time of blackness and hunger
Do not forget us.
Lantern and hay are brought to the ox.

2

Wake us, midnight bell, from our dreaming.
Turn us
From the comfort of the five folded senses.

Let the first unbroken snow
Take the prints of our feet.

We would go out soon
Bearing a sheaf of unlit candles under a cold star.

Did we not always return to the seed sack?
We did not suffer the plough
To languish in the half-broken field
Eaten with the cold fires of rust.

We remembered the black wings
And broke their congregations.

Though late, we sharpened our sickles,
And had a cave
To store a jar of wild honey for the poor.

Therefore, this winter midnight
We will rejoice in The Bread.

GEORGE MACKAY BROWN

Warbeth is a place in Orkney, near Stromness: a monastery stood
there once
To lowse: to unbind, set loose; here used of harvest time when sheaves were
unbound before being fed into the threshing mill

FLOS CAMPI

The rooftree of the year is fallen, fallen
and fallen is the splendour of the grass.
The great trees, barebone senators, observe
gravely the crepuscular season pass.

Here in the stripped pathology of winter
time's bleak agenda lately comes to light;
summer's fluorescence now, and the autumn idyll
matters for hindsight, else an oversight.

This iron season, cloaked in fictive beauty,
the icefield's glory and the blizzard's pride;
and which of us at length has his desire?
or which in having it, is satisfied?

New rose, effulgent, out of time and season
flower of grace on Jesse's ancient tree,
Ah, be the benison of all beginnings,
the steadfast root in our declension be.

KEVIN NICHOLS

STORY

For us there are no certainties, no star
blazing our journey, no decisive dream
to reassure hurt hearts or warn us when
it's time to move. The shepherds, harassed men,
are given answers to the questions they
have never thought to ask. Told where to go
and what to look for. We try out our way
unlit with angels, wondering 'How far?'
Yet in the story we find who we are:
the baby is told nothing, left to grow
slowly to vision through the coloured scheme
of touch, taste, sound; by needing learns to pray,
and makes the way of the flesh, dark stratagem
by which God is and offers all we know.

JENNIFER DINES

HAS NOTHING CHANGED?

The angel of the Lord appeared to Joseph in a dream and said, 'Get up, take the child and his mother and escape to Egypt.' Matthew 2:13

They travelled through the night
Into Egypt, the stars were clear,
As they are now,
The moon was incredibly near,
The mountains rocky,
The way dusty,
As they are now.
There are those who,
For one reason or another,
Travel into Egypt, today.

As the sun came up, cocks crowing,
It would have become hot,
The donkey's head would
Droop lower,
Ears forward, and the mother
Would have drawn
Some shade over the baby's head,
As they do now.

In the desert shimmer
The village they reached
Would have dozed
At midday, the old men squatting
In the shade, and a woman carrying
A water jar on her head
Would have greeted them,
As she greeted me today.

It's a long walk to the well,
And there is no piped water
To this village;
Slowly I seek the shadow of a wall.
Did the small donkey foal
Out on the glittering sand,
Lick its mother's urine
For moisture then,
As it does now?
Has nothing changed, nothing at all?

MARGUERITE WOOD

EXCLUSION

Not in the palaces
    of the Princes
    and the Priests
who live
    by tradition
and kill
    the innocents

But in the homes
    and hiding places
    of the poor
      and persecuted

We find the King
who was born to be
    their Brother

And worship him

SUE ELKINS

THE YOUNG GOATHERD

The three kings rode in majesty,
With myrrh, frankincense, gold:
The shepherds brought a homely gift,
The smallest lamb in fold.

The young goatherd, ragged, thin,
With mischief in his eyes,
Thought, 'Though I have no gifts to bring
I'll give him a surprise.'

The baby saw the lamb and smiled;
It was a furry, new-born thing.
He gave the kings a royal look,
For he too was a king.

The goatherd creeping round the door
Upon his trick intent
Just shouted, 'Bo! I've made you jump,'
Then laughed in merriment.

Shepherds to Shepherd bore their gift
And kings to King deferred,
But from the stable chuckles came;
Bright eyes on that goatherd.

DOREEN WHITTAM

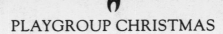

PLAYGROUP CHRISTMAS

Around their leader, chattering,
the playgroup children formed a ring.
There were rowdy Thomas, clever Sue,
Rosie and James, to name a few.

All were tots aged three or four.
Carefree Sunny sat on the floor,
rocking with Teddy, to and fro,
so lovable, but rather slow.

Scraping his chair to make a noise,
Thomas boasted about his toys.
Gentle Jamie described the tree
and opening presents on Dad's knee.

Plump little Rose told of the cakes
and sausage rolls her mother makes.
Susan announced, in a sudden pause,
'I don't believe in Santa Claus.'

Although some kids thought Sunny dim,
he knew what Mum had said to him.
He told them proudly, 'Kissme Day
Is Baby Jeesee's birfyday.'

But no one heard. 'You great fat lump,'
Sue taunted Rose, then what a thump
Tom gave to Sue. 'Stop that my dears,'
the leader said. 'No need for tears.'

She soothed her tots aged three and four,
and carefree Sunny sat on the floor,
rocking with Teddy, to and fro,
so lovable, but rather slow.

DOREEN WHITTAM

INCARNATION

I HAVE SEEN CHRIST

I have seen Christ
in the neglected face of an unloved boy

I have seen Christ
in the gentleness and faith of an old man

I have seen Christ
in the quick hands of a nurse
who knew I needed her before I asked

I have seen Christ
born again in spirit
in the joyful song of a bright-faced child

I have seen Christ
when my heart was breaking
in the compassionate eyes of a friend

I have seen Christ
in the forgiveness of a loved one

I have seen Christ
in the anguish of a mother for her dying son

I have seen Christ
in a dustman and a doctor

God grant
that they may see Christ in me

JOAN ROWBOTTOM

'COME DOWN . . . '

Come down
        from the grand country
you who walk mightily
lower the high hand

Bend low
        come by way
of the hedgerow
where crocus and lily grow

        Here
there is much to see
nothing to fear

Walk quietly by
the sleeping children
quietly be
one with the gentle minded
step down low

Bend low, bend low
where flowers and sleeping children blow

JILL HARRIS

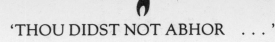

'THOU DIDST NOT ABHOR ...'

'Thou didst not abhor the Virgin's womb'
Nor yet her youthful skin
Stretched to accommodate our God.
'Thou didst not abhor the Virgin's womb'
Nor yet her lungs, her heart, her chemistry.
God — dependent on a woman;
Woman dependent on her God —
Co-existent loveliness,
Hidden lives in Nazareth.

AMY PURDON

THIS STORY

Awake!
I am the Cross
I conqueror destroyer seducer barbarian
I whom it has taken millennia to make and unmake
I, at this juncture of space and time,
One,
Alone
Am
The Cross, the meeting place.
The flame floating in the heart of the bowl
The face peering in the mirror not seeing itself.
The sword and the stone,
The hero and the maiden,
This is I,
This story
This dream
Is all
I.

ALAN JACKSON

INCARNATION

I glimpsed him at the roadside
among urchins in the mud.

His were the hands of a man
at home with craft and wood.

In the drift of dusk and starlight
there was little I understood,

But I saw a beggar woman sleep
on rags on the midden heap.

Hidden behind locked doors
were tight mouths, tight fists.

I saw him smile and turn away.
Wet streets waken in the winter day.

JENNY ROBERTSON

VISITATION

Poetry came bursting in; stood
at the door wild-eyed,
elemental as a savage,
the life-force streaming from his fists;
clenched knuckles of solid bone
banged through the house, the ribs
of the building rattled and bent.
Like thunder incarnate, he
stormed into every room, ripped
down ornaments, tumbled comfort,
terrifying everyone; I
received the gift, as subjects must
accept what rulers give, or live
despoiled; the visit made us pray.
Our fervour was something new —
it matched in awe the energy
that hurled itself upon our home.
Like sunscape of volcanic dust,
repeated day after day,
an unusual beauty settled in my mind.

JOHN BATE

PRAYER

Aimless cars tried to batten on the calm
That fashioned, filled
That pool of stillness in the traffic's noise;
Prayer had time to grow within that church.
Or then within the garden's windswept poise
When swift clouds took their corners at full speed
Merely to sit and let the placid soul
Spread towards God, and many a time within
The chapel hut
When countless raindrops crawled upon the roof
Like millions of live insects, God lifted up
My aimlessness and gave it purpose. Now
It is night-time; a wind runs thru the dark
And raindrops bounce
Upon its surface. All are sleeping here;
Every weary soul lies back and breathes
In peace, and I alone keep watch. The cramped
Hard world of dry and bitter prayer unwinds,
Relaxes, and I talk with God. And now
I know that countless hearts are keeping vigil.
Maybe God is found in the next house
Along the street. The stillness can be touched;
Tables and chairs that listen to the peace,
Are moulded to their own true shape. Prayer can
Be strange; at times we seize upon weak words,
And try to heave and lift them heavenwards,
And yet they choke within our withered mouths;
And this can last for weeks. At other times,
Like now, the single light left on can hear
The dark talk in a low and whispered bass,
And know no fear. Soon I will sleep myself,
Yet night will watch over my quiet bed,
And outside in the dark
The wind will run its comb thru the damp leaves.

RAYNE MACKINNON

EX-CATHEDRA

I would have no stained glass saints in my cathedral
Preferring that there be children of light, always
Active, listening and attentive; I would have no books
Of prayers, torn and shredded at the edges, no old songs,
No plate, chipped pews, bookstall or notice-board,
No thundering status of organ, orators, candles or wands:

But my west window would be the light-patched coat of cloud
Bringing calm after a day's rain; yellow chasing grey,
                              weather clearing to
High light-blue, aerial as a lark, slabbed with reds,
                    sunset-water
And a sound like wind, rippling, running and sighing-over
Beach and channel and shallow sand, lifting the birds, moulding
Sand-rib and dune, pouring out a tide, whistling, changing
As we shall rise, meeting the Lord in the air, becoming
Light as birds, numberless, parents of time, endless.

MARTYN HALSALL

TO DIANA

Watching the cool maternal curve of neck and hair
Beautifully bent over this tiny boy
That is mysteriously you, still unaware
Of self, I let a long tide of content
Wash my mind clean of the old puzzlement,
Of all that is not summed by your own quiet joy.

I think of soft rain out of a long-brazen sky
Breaking the still pain of parched earth;
Of calm on wind-torn seas when tempest die;
Of sun's bright benediction after cold;
The sudden laughter of spring when the year is old,
Spilling from the world's mouth, symphony of rebirth.

These are you, and they are the child too,
As you are the young child and he is you,
For a while longer, breathing your air,
Living only in your warmth, your care.
And flung about you both a nimbus of gold,
A beauty for us to remember when we are old:

The pattern of a mystery to which our sight is dim,
'That he may evermore dwell in us, and we in him.'

MYRA REEVES

POEM TO CHRIST

How is it that at dusk or dawn the pine trees
ravel the pale sky to a pelmet, call
sharply to book our secular certainties
casting into a tenebrous question all
that we in the box of daylight reckoned sound,
walled, housed, secure from the mind's storm?
And which is now the figure, which the ground?
And which the substance here and which the form?

And did you, Roland, penned at Roncesvalles
curling your music up in puffs of sound
to bounce and buffet from the mountain walls,
discriminate note and echo and rebound
and who the singer was and which the song?
And did you, watching the spear's parabola
sort friend from foe, distinguish right from wrong?
Did you between one breath and another breath
mark the sharp frontiers of peace and war
and know which sphere was birth and which was death?

You, little one, washed up by the wave of birth
on to a shore pebbled with uncertainties,
don our contingent flesh upon our earth
to re-establish our realities,
and crack apart the moulds of 'is' and 'seems'
of 'be' and 'not be', waking thought and dreams.
So shall the pine trees calibrate the sky
and demarcate the galaxies that are
moving tonight in a grave harmony;
each tree angled to its particular star.

KEVIN NICHOLS

THE TREE

So, said God, I will lay the edge of my axe
to the root of the tree which I from its beginning
have tenderly cherished; because this tree has proved
perverse and sterile. Year by year I have waited
for the golden fruits of its sap to return
the love I lavished; year by year attended
to the pleas of my gardeners, spare it, spare it.
Yet, after the perennial promise of bud,
leaf, blossom, nothing has it yielded, not even
the bitter crab apple of the wildwood: its only
harvest the rank flowers of evil.
And so I will lay about me. He took his axe,
God, terribly beautiful, the blows rained down
like a firestorm and the wound grew
white and ragged at the head of the roots
where the bole begins, a festering sore.
The hillside rang with the clash of ancient battle
clamorous, smothering almost the cry
shaken out, high and clear from the tall tree
through the tense air saying Abba
Father saying, into thy hands.

KEVIN NICHOLS

JOHN THE BAPTIST

As the brittle water dripped
from the young man standing
upright again to the waist
I heard, we all felt we heard
I saw, we all thought we saw
a visionary presence, a voice;
but where are they gone?

I staked almost everything
on the truth of that moment.
This is the lamb (I blurted out)
the very lamb (or some such phrase)
this is the lamb of God . . . but
that was some years ago.

Now in danger of life, I know
that tyranny will take its course,
and neither the lamb of God nor
anyone else will intervene
to save me.

Where is the hope of his coming?
Was this not the one?
Is the kingdom not after all
at hand?

I waited to see the whole
country rise to his name.
I am waiting

The time is ripe, the world ready
to be reborn, but now

What am I is it the end is he

SIMON BAYNES

THE CALLING OF MATTHEW

What if Our Lord should call
At the Hall
Of Inland Revenue,
And quite without appointment,
Call Matthew from his desk?
Would Matthew check his tax code first,
And claim his pension rights?
Or would he cast aside at once
His tax assessment sheets?
Would Commissioners, aghast,
Enquire the reason why,
Ascribe it all to lunacy?
'Poor fellow's strength is overtaxed;
He's let his work go fly!
Grant sick leave till his mind's relaxed.'
Would colleagues cry: 'What? Straight away!
You know it's overtime till May!'
'Now look here, Matthew!
They'll not like it at the Top.
Questions in the House, you know.'

Matthew answered not at all,
But followed Our Lord,
As he passed unnoticed through the Hall.

FRANK MORLEY

COMMONPLACE

TREASURES

'A man at his end, and at his beginning
Possesses nothing' . . . (This is what's said
At well or smithy, whenever there's word
Of a birth or a death.)
The green hill
Stands guard over the new child.
The burn
Makes him a flute-song.
There are the thousand harps of the sea.
Sun and wind are his friends.
He owns
Grassblades, stars, snowflakes.
(He belongs to them also.)
His the green and golden corn
And the sea's silver, fish,
Which is more
Than the dust-of-gold and sweat-of-silver
On Dives' coat.

Every stone he touches will be precious.
Sound then, harps of the sea.
Green hill, guard a prince.

GEORGE MACKAY BROWN

ST GOVNET, LEAVING INISHEER

A blether of chanting bees on honey sward
about my skep of stone, round cell of silence:
wild angelica, hartstongue that thirsts for streams,
cranesbill shiny and bloody like my Lord.

The long blue bird leans on the topmost course
of wall after wall, chiding the cuckoo farmer
late in sowing, slow in the raking of kelp.
Its soft and solitary yelling 'to sea'

that I must pass over again before I find
the cold and stony place of my resurrection.

One flitting would do me all my days of life.
Here is my hive's bole, this cleft in the rock.
Must I plait grey marram, bind it with split briar
to make once more a travelling box for my bees?

Seething ciborium stopped with balsam, adrift
and angry, swapping its inner store of sweets.
I whisper to them of death as we pass the surf
swing onto ridge and furrow of forageless sea.

I have rubbed their empty house with bedstraw flowers
to summon a wild swarm. My door swings in the wind.

CATHERINE BYRON
*St Govnet is the patron saint of beekeepers: a vision called the saint away
from the island of Inisheer back to the mainland of Ireland, where she
founded a monastery in Co. Cork*

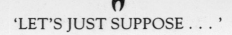

'LET'S JUST SUPPOSE . . . '

Let's just suppose one sunny autumn day
The Eternal Father tipped the heavenly scales
And found humanity worth saving. Think
Just think that good will always win
The struggle against evil. Just suppose
One single spark of human kindness wins
The day, and here, in an old hospital
The angel of the Lord will spread his wings
Over the lost, and all mankind is safe.
Just think Jesus could walk along
The Gorgie Road, and heal the drunks, the drabs.
Christ is alive and sets the blood he shed
Flowing along the veins of tired humanity,
Flushing and filling, ringing, sluicing clean
The doubts, the darkness, and the soul
Immortal rises from the dead, or look
Around and know the unseen dead
Among the bitter roots of grass and rock
Sleep peacefully till at the last great day
The Cross of Shame will shine renewed among
The joyous constellations, and the sky
Crack into cataracts of light. Perhaps
Even the Pharisees with their hard
Hunger after righteousness would feel
The heavenly fields of wondering wheat
Will feed the resurrected.
And the invisible and hidden God
Will shine renewed,
And gather the exhausted planets, stars
Into his arms.

But who can fathom the Almighty's ways?
Slowly the vision fades, and I am back
Again in stale Ward Ten — ashtrays full
Of stale tobacco, broken chairs, nearby
The TV talking sleepily to itself.
Now peace returns, and for half an hour, it seems
What was a Hell becomes a Haven once more.

RAYNE MACKINNON

THE VISITOR

Twice,
that sleety twilit afternoon
I glanced up sharply from the ironing
and saw, out in the dismal garden,
beyond the thickening window
our reluctant great-tit,
persuaded by winter's argument
towards the pendulous, swinging coconut; —

almost as if the Lord,
temporarily leaving aside weightier matters
had quietly entered the room
and tapped me on the shoulder,
saying

Do look, don't miss him,
isn't he wonderful?
Put down that shirt, just for a moment,
and join in my delight,
for I love you even as I love him,
and I want you to share my pleasure
in this tiny ruffled topknot
of my Creation,

pecking at life's cold shell
cupped in my wide hands; —

and tasting joy.

JAN GODFREY

APRIL SUNLIGHT: KITCHEN MUSE

Today, the sun is lord; banishing the commonplace.
Crocks and cupboards, pots and pans — all aglow
With borrowed brilliance. And I have moved in a fret of shining
As palpable as rain, plying my kitchen craft
With a heart lightened, soothed by the tender touch
Of sudden summer. Today I have known serenity.

And I think of Julian . . . and her words.
Perhaps it was on a day like this,
Busy with tasks like these,
That her heart was sure;
'All shall be well and
All manner of thing shall be well.'

Outside, bloom and blossom stir and dapple in lazy silence.
A flurry of petals falters down from the apple-tree
To tesserate the grass in pallid patterns.
A special beauty I feel in the fall of petals,
And a parable of hope . . . that dying may be gentle
And death rebirth.

ALICE FAIRCLOUGH

from SERMON ON MIDLENT SUNDAY

All art is a parable of eternity.
There is no poet who believes in the victory of dumbness
no painter who sees the eternal death of colour;
Beethoven rises in the fiery flight of eternal music.
The singer hears within the perfect song
therefore such songs must be.
But you have built with strawless bricks of logic
an asylum whose gleaming walls
reflect the barren madness of your thought.

Turn your eyes away from hedging your bets,
the financial pages and the bank-balance,
the hope of tasting a last glutted luxury
before the crab or the coronary,
the cry in the dark: thou fool
tonight thy soul shall be required of thee.

In the dark night that links sleeping and rising
when the whole house is stilled,
seek to discover in that silent time
the lost alternative: in the end all shall be well
all manner of thing shall be well.

WILLIAM NEILL

LENT

Lent is a tree without blossom, without leaf,
Barer than blackthorn in its winter sleep,
All unadorned. Unlike Christmas which decrees
The setting-up, the dressing-up of trees,
Lent is a taking down, a stripping bare,
A starkness after all has been withdrawn
Of surplus and superfluous,
Leaving no hiding-place, only an emptiness
Between black branches, a most precious space
Before the leaf, before the time of flowers;
Lest we should see only the leaf, the flower,
Lest we should miss the stars.

JEAN M. WATT

LENTEN EVENING, MAYNOOTH

Air ice cool;
Legions of spears thrust up from chestnut trees,
Dark against the late light,
Advance guard alert.

Sky gold mauve,
cold colour-washed banner;
Lenten violets' purple deepen
Shrouded by dusk.

Sun slips down;
Blackbird chinks his curfew call.
Ashen moon sharpens and shines
Darkening the shadows.

Trees loom large,
Ghostly grey, cathedral strong,
Bastions well-tried and seasoned
Stand and listen.

Dark drifts in
Escaping the extending fingers of day;
Spring retreats from night
Biding time.

Everything waits.
Silently the power of life gathers strength
Waiting to shout out victory.
'Christ is risen!'
Alleluia!

SISTER PAMELA STOTTER

FOR MY FRIENDS

Spendthrift friendships once ravelled and unravelled,
Carefree, leisurely as a journey without a plan;
Easy-come, easy-go, there was a while I travelled
Lightly, made my friends catch-as-catch-can.
Gradually, the casual twisted the precious weave,
This tissue of feeling in which I have grown;
Though I follow a single thread, I must believe
That bound to the whole we never drift alone.
Crossed, matted as fibres long inwrought,
Friendships prove the fabric of a common story,
The web which takes the strain of every thought,
Shares the fray or stain, joys in our glory.
Interwoven, at last I dare to move without misgiving;
I touch the invisible, love this gauze of living.

MICHEAL O'SIADHAIL

LUNCHTIME IN A LONDON CAFE

Table by table the cafe fills
Till talk and the clap of plates
Bulge with well-being; a dark
Waitress' patchwork skirt
Hurries behind the counter;
Every face under the sun peers
At the window menu, more
Voices join the steamy pentecost.

Here in the metropolis nothing
Shocks. Out of its huge anonymity
Worlds of strange gossip crowd
This lunchtime cafe. And I'm in love
With its mystery, the peculiar rapture
Of life à la carte. The window mists;
After wine, the Basque in the corner
Turns his smoky eyes on the waitress.

Outside the door, the buses shriek,
Rush and judder; a city's jamboree,
Hope and haphazard, limitless
Chances, choices wait. Sitting
Here I know I've felt the throb
Of Jerusalem or Rome or any city
Yet to come, where there's a cafe
And we, citizens all, break bread.

MICHEAL O'SIADHAIL

FOR DOLLY

Light as a bird,
quick, shy and busy as a woodmouse,
little handmaid of the Lord
with soft brown hair
and timeless porcelain features,
who comes early morning and after school
to watch the milking, feed lambs,
gather brown eggs, still warm, like treasures,
and joy in the wonder of it.
Child-woman, ten years old,
mothering your baby sisters,
cradling the she-cat,
turning handstands under the plum-blossom
and playing house, secretly,
in the barn-loft.

JOAN ROWBOTTOM

TELEPHONE CONVERSATION

(first kiss)

Some appear full length
before me, when they talk.
(My mother, tall and thin
in the crackling distance.)
Others are portraits.
(A great aunt, sitting
as for an artist;
I see her hat, pearls,
the bowl of flowers.)
There is the business pose
of passport size and scope.
When planning times together
my friends have action shots,
the focal length dependent on
the game we fix.

You were startling,
grainy, black and white,
so close that I could see
only your mouth, your chin,
tomorrow's beard speckling
the surface. Your voice so near
that when we next met
to kiss you, hero of an old film,
was almost replay.

ROSEMARY A. HECTOR

TULIPS AT THE WINDOW

Tulips lean in crystal vase;
oval leaves, cool glass support
reluctant buds, which open slowly
coaxed by coal-fire warmth.
Burdened with the ripening
beauty of their flowers
the stern stems bend; full petals fall.
Only one tight-wrapped remains,
north facing, where cold light
cannot entice, but only try to prise
its secret bloom.

ROSEMARY A. HECTOR

WASHING DAY

Socks and stockings
are strung like crotchets on the line.
White shirts trill a little
beside the trumpeting of
underwear let loose.
Sheets clap, trousers flap,
dishcloths drip in time.
They have come to expect
this ritual of song and dance:
fabric from my world inside.

ROSEMARY A. HECTOR

LAUGHTER
AND TEARS

HAIR 543 . . .

Hair 54329635 fell out today.
God noticed.

JOAN BROCKELSBY

TEARS

'Better sadness than laughter', Ecclesiastes 7:3

Who, knowing tears, can be content with laughter?
They wear slowly,
a thin hosing of water, that slides
down the exposed surfaces of rocks,
smoothing them, making runnels in the hard stone,
and sometimes, moaning in the reinforcement of storm,
rushing in floods to the swelling rivers,
picking pebbles and muds, to race them round
and round in suddenly formed deep pools.
Laughing we forget those who cannot laugh,
but weeping we make a communion.
Tears will soak us through the soil,
down into high, silent caves, where sadness
losing all its sharpness is as soft as air,
and we can bathe naked in the still waters,
sharing unashamedly with other naked folk,
the ravages that brought us there.

JOHN BATE

VE DAY, 1945

Thrang, thrang's the fowk in the wide city,
But my luve's nae there.
My luve is won awa frae ilka ditty,
He daunces at nae fair.
O harp, ye harpers, while I climb upward at even
By my auld wearie stair.
The sun bends doon, the lavrock comes hame frae heaven
But my luve nae mair.

OLIVE FRASER

*This is one of five poems in Scots by Olive Fraser which won an Arts
Council Competition for poems in Scots in 1951.*

GLOSSARY. *Thrang,* crowded; *fowk,* folk; *nae,* not; *won awa frae,*
escape from, get free of; *ditty,* song, but also *dittay,* Scots Law,
indictment, accusation — my love has escaped from guilt, sorrow,
shame, etc; *lavrock,* skylark.

FALLING STAR

*For my brother Stephen, who committed suicide, aged 27, by jumping from
a hospital window*

Bright star tarnished, you were always
set for the edge of the universe, but never in orbit;
you span and span on your own dark spot
sent out wild flashes of white fire

while I, stargazer, wept each night
for your trackless brilliance,
your glittering all to no end

till, turned inward, you burned out
in your own blaze of glory,
exploded like a planet

hit the edge of the universe, and God's white fire

VERONICA ZUNDEL

CONUNDRUM

If I drop two oatcakes out of a fifth-floor window.
    while waving goodbye to a gentle friend
    who is on his way to India to find himself,
    and at the same time trying to snatch a quick bite
    before returning to my life's work entitled:
    'How To Get On Top Without It Getting You Down,'

and

if one of the oatcakes falls into a sleeping baby's pram,
    bashing its innocent nose to such an extent
    that the nose bleeds and the baby yells

and

    if the other oatcake should knock a kingsize into the pram
    from out of the hand of a passing fourteen year old punk

and

    if the mother who was up to her knees in dirty dishes
    she using the old-fashioned method
    rushes out to find the punk rummaging in the pram
    for his lost solace while her baby cries
    with a bleeding battered nose

and

if the said aggrieved and much careworn mum jumps instantly
    and forgiveably to the wrong conclusion
    and yanks the punk by the hair meanwhile bawling
    and shouting at him

and

if he, being a stranger both to the art of articulate speech
    and the legends of the Knights of the Round Table,
    kicks her in the legs

and

if she, being immensely stronger and much angrier
    than any young amateur of anarchism
    drags him pell-mell round the corner to get justice

and

if meanwhile the wind, picking up a little, begins
    to fan the smouldering Rothman's as it nestles
    in the warm woollies of the howling babe

and

if also the plastic nappies of the babe are highly combustible
so that the rosy-cheeked one is soon the centre of a raging
    inferno and is with rather shocking speed reduced to cinders,
    not to mention the pram and it not paid for yet

well

I mean, am I to blame, am I to blame?
    Myself, biased though I may be, I think not,
    personally and without overly exercising myself,
    I blame my friend who went off to India,
    frankly.

ALAN JACKSON

ADAM

It wasn't me
it was that woman
she doesn't know what's good for her
she did it

and then
it was that snake
slimy horrible snake
I wouldn't have believed a word
I wouldn't have been taken in
imagine a talking snake
well I ask you

and then
and then
it was *you*
you gave me Eve
you made the serpent
it's your rotten apple
you knew all about it —
I was miles away
doing the garden like I was told
you're the one
you did it
it wasn't me
it *wasn't* me

and anyway I only took a little bite

GODFREY RUST

BAD POEM ABOUT BALAAM

Balaam was big headed and Balaam behaved badly
By being too big to Moabites and other pushed up princes.
Too big he was for Saxone's size six boots,
So God told Balaam's ass to rock him to the roots
And bring him back from being such a big head bore.
So Balaam's ass stopped short and Balaam's boot got caught.
She banged his boot a wallop on the wayside wall.
Then you should have heard how bumped up Balaam bawled.
Bad Balaam beat his ass a thumping crack
But she called back, condemned his cruel attack:
'You've beat me Balaam, bruised my bony back —
Your size six boots will surely have to walk.'
Now Balaam never knew his ass could talk.
It brought him out in sweat and rocked his ankles rigid.
Inside his size six boots his toe nails curled to their roots,
And shrunk his big head back to better size.
Which shows that when you wear a big head's shoe,
And brag at being big with pagan pushed up princes
And wash your hair and powder wigs with expensive rinses —
Your ass may show some better sense than you.

CHRIS PORTEOUS

RONEO AND JULIET

We met in the
Xerox copy shop,
each looking for
enlargements.
Her face
was my type
and I hoped she might
duplicate
my feelings,
but while I had it down
in black and white
it soon became transparent
she brought only
a handful of negatives,

so seeing
there could be no
developments
I left,
wondering if
some day her
prints will come
prints will come
prints will come
prints will come.

GODFREY RUST

THE GATE

When they moved into the house he said
'I'll fix that creaking gate one day.'
In later years he changed his tune —
'Creaking gates hang longest — look at me!'
She came to love the gate, it told her things,
told her when he was coming home.

       After the funeral her son said
       'I'll get that gate replaced, Dad
       never got round to it.'

The new gate is silent, swings smooth
on oiled hinges, closes
with a well-ordered click,
but the music has gone out of her life
and she is left with a feeling of betrayal.

R.P. FENWICK

THOUGHTS OF A CHRISTIAN TURNED FIFTY

The score is not impressive
my boots pinch
but I am still on the field
muddy but unbowed.
With so many missed chances
bungled tackles
and own goals
it is a wonder my manager
has not yet called me in.
But here I am
into the second half
under the glare of the crowd
keeping my captain
in the corner of my eye.
Sometimes even now
passes come my way.
Steady it.
There is of course the cup.
I hope the whistle
will find me pressing
towards the goal.

SIMON BAYNES

IMPERFECTION

Though crude, the market pottery at Turda
Was perfect: Chagall's cocks
Not more so. Had we not taken that moment
We should have lost such perfection,
for in returning, organized, at ease
with friends, the stall had gone.
(We never saw the attendant potter.)
Instead, I photographed the country folk,
Seeking their innermost forms.
But what seemed completed then
Was nothing. The film had not wound on,
and we bought something else instead.

That was a deceptive town, that Turda.
I thought, in coming to it first,
That we had lost the best scenery,
Were left with a cement factory and its dust.
But beyond were more hills and better.

DAVID BARRATT

CHRIST CHILD

It was the summer holiday,
— well, holiday for some.
You knocked at the door, stained and weary
from the day's heat, and I remember
your blue eyes and dusty face,
and blond hair, and plimsolls.

You said, could you wash the car,
or any other job, for money?
I didn't mind the money, but the thought
of what you'd do with it.
You must be far from home already,
— I've never seen you here before.

Does your mother know
where you are, and that you're by yourself?
Summer is the time for playmates,
not for wandering alone
in strange neighbourhoods,
asking at the door for money.

I couldn't just say 'No',
We sat under a tree in the garden
while you had a drink;
and the look in your eyes
said you'd rather have love than money,
if only you knew what it was.

Why did you want the money?
You said, 'To go to the city.'
It was four o'clock, and nearly time for tea.
'Wouldn't yours be ready soon?'
'No.' There'd be no one back till seven.
And you'd been wandering since breakfast.

I asked you where you lived.
You suddenly withdrew
and made to go, with a look
inexpressible in words.
My conscience watched till you were out of view,
and you never turned back, once.

You said your name was Paul.
It could have been any name,
or no name, it's all the same —
names are for people who belong to someone.
You were just a wanderer,
moving on because I mentioned home.

My suburban patch became an accusation,
and my thoughts dwelt for longer
than was comfortable, on the other half
and how they lived. Council house or terrace,
doesn't matter what, so long as there is love,
and Mum to get the tea.

Your face stayed with me, would not go away.
It seemed that it was Christ
looking through those eyes,
and suffering, his agony unfinished,
for a world that does not love even children
with innocent and sad blue eyes.

I thought you might come back again.
I prayed for you,
but it didn't seem enough.
How does Jesus answer prayer?
Only by the love we show
for one another in his name.

It's Easter now, and holidays once more.
where are you, Paul? God forbid
that it would happen
to a child of mine.
Oh Christ, let someone plant a seed of love
this spring, in that child's garden.

JOAN ROWBOTTOM

THREE A.M.

Nuns keep vigil with psalm and measured voice;
nurses manoeuvre amidst moans and snores.
Racked against the long-drawn, ticking night,
dry-mouthed, driven from sleep, I wait;
imagine in each bang and engine noise
the overdue return, the rasping key;
get up, grope for his empty bed, and pray
no less devoutly than devoted soeurs —
as anxiously as nurses watch for day.
Morning is now four short hours away.
The wind blows litter over silent streets.
Dossers and drunks find huddled brief respite,
and junkies dream gaunt nightmares. My fears
fuse with relief and fury: the boy appears.

JENNY ROBERTSON

LANDSCAPE

FENSCAPE

after winter rain the enormous sky
opens blue eyes in wet-lashed wonder

at its own shattered reflection
a blink a breath caught held in

cracked ice mirrors, thin light
fingering heaven's seamless hem of

broken clouds spilling colour into
painted pools of living moving water

shining turquoise puddles scooped from
pumpernickel earth's harsh richness of

clumbered furrows, black bones converging
to a narrow ribbed sharp-cut perspective

hardly peopled or housed this iron bleakness
broken tree scarecrow-man land taut to

time's horizon; mocked pecked he stands
dumb wooden guardian of all our innocences

as a man once swung between the heavens
and all the frozen darkened earth.

JAN GODFREY

CELTIC CHAPEL

A rusted grating in the ancient wall
in whose cold squares the child would frame his face;
the roofless gables held their light and space
where monks came singing to the vesper call.

This, they said, used to be the home of God,
this fading whisper of an ancient tale.
A silent chantry without altar rail,
bare ruin reaching for the sailing cloud.

WILLIAM NEILL

CHURCH HISTORY

Recall the roofless kirk where Ringan prayed,
the bones of singers in the ancient yard.
After the smashing zealots locked the gate
where superstitious ghosts might keep their ward.

Still beehive monks chant a goidelic lay
in the dark nave of schooled imagination;
a contrast to the elders' tailored grey
defining bounds to transubstantiation.

Pulpit direction marks what is, is not:
decently keeps a subtler darkness hid.
The older mysteries are more surely caught
behind this crumbling wall and bolted grid.

WILLIAM NEILL

A HIGHLAND TESTIMONY

We had our ritual too. Down the long glen,
While startled curlews cried on ebb-tide sands,
We all would walk, our Bibles in our hands,
And winter sunshine turned to rain again.

The crisp and cutting edge of our dark suits
Served as a weekly penance. We, in turn,
Would kick some chuckies into ditch or burn,
And scuff the polish on our Sunday boots.

The church bell spread its iron news abroad,
Dull through the trees or clear across the bay.
With quickened step we hastened on our way.
And so we entered in the house of God.

Thus went the ritual of that far-off day.
The creak of bell and bell-rope clanged and jarred.
The psalms were dignified. The pews were hard.
The rain was soft. The lowering skies were grey.

Grey too the tenor of our world today.
The death of humanism, sick and sad.
And I could wish that once again we had
That child's acceptance of the Christian way.

Faith of my fathers. If it came again,
I would not change a moment of my youth,
The grey kirk and the straight unflinching truth,
Clean as the stones at the burn-side in the glen.

ALISTAIR HALDEN
This poem won the Scottish Open Poetry Competition, 1985

APRIL 16TH

Trees do not grow
for three or four years
after being transplanted.
They settle their roots.

These trees in the park
are large to have been uprooted.
The younger the tree
the quicker it settles and grows;
so I am told.

My experience is different.
Roots were dragging me under.
I could not grow for the heavy clinging.

Transplanted now
I am lifted, winging,
weightless almost.

My growing is to shed
all that holds me down.

I grow stems of thought
to flower as poems.

TESSA RANSFORD

JOHN CLARE'S JOURNEY

John Clare's journal recalls a boyhood journey to try to find the edge of the world. As he came home, half his village was out, searching for him.

Earth quivers in the heat, the level light
Locks the square heath, limits the horizon-wall;
Eye follows far as the furze, sees clapper-sun
Simmering within the purled hood of its sound.

All this he notes, the land being lower to a boy,
Its edge less far, half a day's walk or less;
He sets out, printing the dust around the gorse,
His legs collecting pollen like a bee.

Noon brings him to new silence, nothing found;
Always, as he ambles on, the edge precedes him;
He finds crouched trees, hears the odd gust of birdsong,
The dry mechanics of a million hidden grasshoppers —

And this is part of silence, become new sound,
Changing, as he listens, to breathing surf below him,
The crackle of hurled spray-sheets strangely torn,
Eddy of air in the throat of the cliffs' cauldron

Boiling, as his giddy eyes rove in the gorge
That is the world's edge, watching, some miles below,
The gliding spans of seabirds turn among
Seabreakers ending life, cloudland being born.

Marvelling, he rises from cramped shade, takes heat
Like a swimmer breasting tideflow, striking out;
Only the lizard on the crumbled rock
Absorbs the afternoon: all hawks rest.

He hears, from everywhere as he nears home.
His name flared out like marsh-grass in the dusk —
'John Clare!' — his father's hand, his mother's tears
Punish and wonder at his wandered absence.

Years later, those who pass the high, spiked wall,
Where visions clamour as he pours sweet tea,
Say: 'We remember the day that sent him here,
That sunlight singed his mind; later he wrote strange things.'

MARTYN HALSALL

John Clare (1793–1864): son of a Northamptonshire labourer, herd-boy, soldier, vagrant, unsuccessful farmer and poet, author of poems of rural life, including The Shepherd's Calendar. *Suffered from mental illness and in 1837 was admitted to Northampton County Asylum, the setting for one of his much-anthologized poems.*

THE SICK ARTIST IN WINTERTIME

Snow-miracle, that over man's ugliness lays
(bird-bath and bungalow, grim grey and ghastly greenhouse)
white amice of godlike redemption and alike over Nature's
treasures redundantly draws its smangle-encrusted creation.

Brash soldier of snow now, black labrador uprightly prances,
all fool unawares, on the sky, its camouflaged silhouette,
as flurrying snow, tail flaring, Pekinese
romps wintersport through the footfalls' dip and delve;
above, ham actor that covets a starring role,
off-white, old seagull circles, whilst below
snow-blossomed trees freeze starlings' torpid twitter,
their stained glass shapes upon sky's amber lights
in branches' quadrilaterals bleakly painted.

Fine spinnies of snow are blown, like smoke, from rooftops,
curling and dissipating, whilst around
flurries the inconstant downdrift undirected,
subject to gusts and eddies (painters here
make snowscapes wrong scapes, painting slants and whirls
of same-size spots, but never is this so.

Showering into your face or windows fling,
perspective-subject — near, large, then smaller-getting,
now large again, and then to smallest point
tirelessy, teasingly, diminishing and advancing
in unrehearsed and Isadorean frenzy,
assorted spots their twisting tarantellas).

Unerringly, alone, the Japanese painters render
perspective in snow, no doubt seeing more than they care to!

Sun sets on the foot-flat snow then, all glory and glitter,
on the green-glass-hardened slopes, child cheer and pensioner peril
as, back of the dusking station grimly poles through
ice the lovely lined-faced Christopher bearing
his grey-green love-load, baby-capped now with snow.

Craves painter's craft all, but with grief for me,
default now painter's strength, though not his art,
word-pictures alone can diffident frame. But is there
not also snow-death, that over man's ugliness lays
white alb of our Christ's salvation, his failures and fears
Love's sheets of a terminal healing? Since I know this is so,
or summer or winter, O times how I long for snow.

DENNIS CORBYN

THE GLEN OF THE CLEARANCE

1   Now the snows come to mass
And the white hares like ghosts pass.
Asperges me, Domine.

2   Wing and web behold the sky
And the wan whimbrel doth cry
'*Et clamor meus ad te veniat.*'

3   No fire shineth nor door doth stand.
The reed prayeth in the land
'*Exaudi nos, Domine.*'

4   No lamp showeth nor foot doth fall
And our fathers sleep, below the wall.
Kyrie eleison.

5   No sweet child here doth sing
But the poor lark to his King
'*Gloria in excelsis Deo.*'

6   And blinded bourne, fading field
Whisper where dormouse and owlet bield
'*Vitam venturi saeculi.*'

7   Land of our love, how thou did'st shine
Land of my heart, O never mine
Dum recordaremur tui, Sion.

8   Thou, not I, thou silent place
Shalt speak this last word for my race,
Sacrificium vespertinum.

9   'O Clan Domnuill, who shall rouse
      The fire in the fallen house,
      Flamman aeternae caritatis?

10   'Children of storm, who yet did see
      In the guest the Blessed Trinity,
      Redime me, et miserere mei.

11   'O Clan of Sim, whose ghosts yet light
      Thy poet in the world's night
      Quorum memoriam agimus in terris.

12   'Feet of your children, did they but pass
      The stones would shout in this frore grass
      "Sursum corda".

13   No voice answers. The great deer tread
      Over the lands of the dead,
      Et dormiunt in somno pacis.

14   The peregrine has his eyrie above,
      But the children of Domnuill the world rove
      Dimitte nobis debita nostra.

15   The hill hawk's eyas is cradled there,
      But the children of Sim where no man doth care.
      Libera nos a male.

16   The hill hawk's eyas beholds from heaven
      Where the bread of children to dogs was given.
      Libera nos, quaesumus, Domine.

OLIVE FRASER

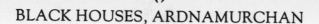

BLACK HOUSES, ARDNAMURCHAN

Displaced from green glens
by the greed of their landlords,
they lived here beside
a seascape of islands,
burrowing close to bog and rock
in a huddle of houses,
where women tended hearth, cradle, deathbed,
bore peats, boulders, bairns, buckets of water.
Men laid well-set lintels, fashioned space
for fire, for hinges; wrestled with rock,
turned windswept ground into lazybed:
their speech, their resourcefulness despised by their landlords
whose calculated rapacity swept them still further
in shiploads.

No funerals here for them, no names in the kirkyard.
Only the stones they once fitted together
stand empty and roofless,
a lament without language,
harsh as the cry of seagull and raven.

JENNY ROBERTSON

CORNERS

Light is cornered here
by astragals, brass plaques and handles,
square, in the New Town manner.
These angles are so right;
they split and rule the streets,
plot and piece not only pavements,
but even carve the very air to blocks.
This enlightened space
knows no mystery;
fronts infer both backs and sides,
dimensions predictable,
sliced and spiked by railings.

Old Town corners are for kissing in,
where air is gathered in, and fog collects
and lingers, or draughts whistle,
lift the skirts of tripping office girls.
They are the remnants of old space
which piecemeal minds forgot to fill,
embraced by buildings
we forgot to fell.

ROSEMARY A. HECTOR

THE BREAKING HEART OF SIMONE WEIL

So it is
In coming to a Portuguese village
At the feast of the local saint,
The women singing a sorrowful song
Of the empty sea, the sea breaking
Upon the shore, and the women
Silhouettes in a stark moonlight
That happens when the earth blocks
The sun, the sun and the moon
In opposition, and the tide high,
The procession of candle-bearing
Women imploring protection for their men
And their boats from a sea
Without ears, and their singing
In contradiction with the brute
Uncaring sea, that it happens:
The irreconcilable breaks the heart
Of a stranded shadow watching
Alone, with the brand of the factory
Slave burned deep in her soul.

It is the cross, an intolerable
Helplessness that rends the soul,
Making the absence of God felt
Through the shock of received beauty
Which shatters the chains of the Cave,
Leaving the freed slave to stumble
Up through a world of half-dreams and
Real sufferings, thirsting for a religion
Of love, and inconsolable bitterness.
One uninterrupted cry
In the eternal silence.

K. LLOYD-THOMPSON

MOROCCAN JOURNEY

There are more beggars
in Marakesh
clinging like limpets
to the tourists
drawn like moths to a flame
by the click of shutters
the whirr of motordrives.
Old young blind
crying 'Allah'
holding empty plastic
washing-up bowls
heavenwards
waiting for the rain
of sight-seers derams.
And the haggard face
with a scorpion
on the nose and snake
around the neck
doing photocalls for
coppers.
      Folk artists
regaling an audience
of English speakers
with their legends
the pennies trickle
into an upturned
drum.

We swim in this sea, pushing them aside
like debris, swearing at them in French,
in firm schoolmaster French 'Non pas
d'argent. Rien.' It is a lie.
It is written in their eyes in neon
that they know you for what you are
Those called blessed and looked upon
as special channels of grace are
refuse, blots on a tourist map.

The scorpion does not move. But the old man
thrusts a sandsnake at the camera, laughing
'picture, picture. Lovely snake.' And the kids
with drums haggle over derams
                              while the gap-toothed
conjuror with the pitted face slips the snake's head
into his mouth.
                    It is hard to focus and frame the face
to gain maximum impact on the page, the pity dwarfed
by compulsion to get it all on celluloid.
He laughs. From his empty belly he laughs. From his
rattling soul he laughs and laughs. And the fool
with the telephoto, worrying over his exposure,
doesn't see the joke.

SIMON JONES

SAINT CATHERINE'S MONASTERY

It is a place of bones.
Catherine's herself
lie safely fleshless
shrined in a blue box
in her own chapel.

Martyred in the desert
a monastery grew round
her skeleton
dry bones
sprouting a place of pilgrimage
a place of cypresses and olives
green in the wafer-dry peninsular
that holds out its thirsty tongue
to lap the salt of the Red Sea.

For a thousand years
there have been monks
Greek-speaking, black-clad
drawn by some divining rod of vocation
to this source of water in the desert.

Here in this whitewashed room
are heaped the skulls
of a millennium of them
lining the walls, filling the cupboards
piled in untidy mounds on the floor
grimy calcium masks
with their gape of eye sockets
grin of mouths
each one exhumed and here exhibited
anonymous, having lost below earth
that skin that was the colour of rock at sunrise
and the eye brown as a fresh date
the black ringlet threaded with a silk of white hair
the crinkle which the smile carved.

It is a place where bones are casually shown
where they have become as normal
as the scant rockiness of landscape
which is all the eye has to look upon.

It is the monastery's grapefruit tree
it is the fact of the pilgrims
or of one of the monks
offering cups of sweet tea
and biscuits flavoured with herbs
which in this strip of earth
is rarity, is miracle.

·ELIZABETH BURNS

This poem won first prize in the Edinburgh City Poetry Competition, 1987

DURHAM CATHEDRAL

At first it was a holy site,
placed in a winding river's loop,
mapped with a gaudy asterisk,
'Cathedral' in the key.
Later Man produced a surplus
to invent a God;
tectonic miracles stood
to His attention.
Then strange cocktails
of theology poured
from the Bishop's room
(a conservation zone).

After all that learning
was recessed in my brain,
a journey south had cause to
take me through this learnt,
but unknown place.
The night-train paused;
I groped for facts and dates,
theories, themes and conquests;
then saw the spotlit stone
tall, above the darkness
of my ignorance.

ROSEMARY A. HECTOR

ABBEY

Fixed on the hard, high cliff, a welcome-home
from the moors' hill or the changing sea;
stiff-backed, guarding the inheritance, joining
memory to memory, seeking to secure.

Run back the chain of time, heavy
with the silenced speech of sixty generations.
Here, at the first, a kingly vow was paid
to the throne of God by this gift
of land to a holy woman; she building
with splintered wood and spirit's stones.
A tuneless cowherd sung a song
that heaven gave, and long-garbed innocence
chanted its crisp new faith in the morning air.

The day of the pioneers was past;
    the blast of centuries,
    the hand of the invader,
    shook what was known;
and these familiar stones
were raised in hopes to praise God
    by the sweat of men.
    Sand trickled through the hour-glass,
    coins through the fingers;
    and soon the mumbled creed
    was scarcely heard
    as the chalice tumbled
    and the goblet filled,
lulling to the drowsiness of noon.
sudden horses' hooves
brought news of the king's edict:
    the plunder would begin.

In the gloom, the rain smacks down,
further to green the grassy floor; the wind
rips through the empty cloisters, pillaging;
plays furious games in the glassless tracery.

HAZEL PALMER

CAEDMON

Peddling music from the edges of the west,
an Irish pauper with a sack of songs,
patched tatters brave as Easter daffodils,
came to the convent, and the harp went round.

The cowherd slipped away from supper,
the meal half done, still hungering among
his beasts, whose lowing seemed less tuneless than
his own discordant humming, for he loved to sing
and music pulsed in him like winter waves
breaking on Whitby's cliffs,
yet rasped like shingle in his throat.

An angel blazing stars and cobwebs
shone that night in Caedmon's cowshed. 'Sing!'
Afraid, the serf stammered assent, returned
to supper amidst much laughter, seized
the harp, and baptised flat Saxon vowels
with flooding tides of sound.

A monkish pen remarked on curling parchment:
'This herdsman excelled the most skilled minstrel,
although from birth tone deaf and singing dumb.'

JENNY ROBERTSON

THE RAID

Our bird-prow breasted ocean bite
eight days and nights.
We made new landfall
at a grassy island
lying some half-league off
a coast of broad white sand.

There found a stone burgh,
tended for some absent lord
by silent, black-smocked men;
they ran before our first attack,
no weapon coming to their hands.
We cut them down in fields,
on sand, and even cowering
on their knees within the darkness
of the great stone barn.

A few had put to sea
in small boats, but we let them go;
all they took with them
was a wooden box of bones,
— or so the captives swore.
This was poor sport —
and not one woman found
in any corner of the island.

Even their treasure hoard was meagre,
— one gold cup, a little coin,
the rest just skin and parchment,
sheets and bundles everywhere
scratched over with the never-ending
black runes of their scribe.

What sheep our boats would carry
we drove off, then fired
the buildings, drank their wine,
consoled each other
this had been the easiest
day's work we'd ever known.

Yet always afterward
a feeling haunts me
that we rowed for home
leaving behind us, unaware,
some greater wealth they owned.

TONY LUCAS

VIKING FLUTE, YORK

The first cold shaft of light
wakens the bay.
Far in the east a sail gleams,
A swan stirs. Soon wingbeats slice the sky.

Time out of mind lost heroes are seen returning
unrecognized,
unless by a single flute, a solitary songbird.
Gaunt minstrels prepare their tale.

Music is central. Stories wait to be gathered
like stones washed high by winter tides,
shaped by storm winds.

So central is music that when the swan
nears the pillaging ship
one bow twangs purposeful discords.

Like a drum's dull thud the bird lands.
Wings thrash the wooden deck
as if in defiance of death.

There is no beauty in this killing.
There is no art in death,
but from the mute swan's wing bone,
finger thin, Yorsen carves
a flute, and bores two holes for breath and feeling.

Now the dead bird's still bone sings.
Music attracts grey seals, and speeds the ship
to a wide estuary, straw-thatched huts,
a wooden minster.

Yorsen, who cannot write,
plies his flute as scribes their pens:
scrawls sagas, sings yarns,
filters drifts of sound soft as down
and describes with lip and finger
the bright flight of a swan.

JENNY ROBERTSON

THE ICON

Our lane has led its cornfields to a swell
that passes here for height, and now we stand
a few feet up and watch the tethered land
escape to distance. You muse how
to comprehend it with an artist's skill;
for what could centre these blond acres? Such
continuous flowing makes you think of Dutch
landscapes, but whose brush could dare that now?

It might be done by opposites, perhaps:
a foil for cloudscapes; an Old Master's ploy
of loving miniature to tempt the eye
into a countryside beyond the Cross.
But where's the subject for our miles of flax
and beet and barley and small woods? No tree
stands grand enough, not even this free
dancing ash, itself harmonious

(music we think may be the clearest form);
and farms are much too scattered and too few,
the one low church-tower only half in view,
and hedgerows all the same. The eye must rest
and so returns to where we stand, the warm
lane at our feet, intent small lives that dart
startled into grass. Yet here my heart,
shocked into recognition, ends the quest.

Our icon now, a grass-snake in the sun
lies in a love-knot passing wheels have ironed
dead on the camber, carelessly refined
to polished pewter, a fixed harmony
that centres all. As once round such a one,
hammered and still, so now begin to turn
the fields and farms, slowly begin to turn
the low gold world, the great cloud-acred sky.

JENNIFER DINES

BEATITUDE

THE GUARDIANS

May a strong guardian
Stand at the door
With sword and olive branch.

May the keeper of the windows
Be eager-eyed
For dawn and the first star,
       snow-light and corn-light.

May the keeper of the fire
See a loaf on the table
And faces of travellers lit with welcome
       and shadow-of-flame, in winter.

May the keeper of the beds be resolute
Against the terror that walks by night,
And herd with gentleness the flocks of sleep.

In a blue-and-silver morning
On the first winter step
Those guardians, and others who hold
       a finger to the lip, smiling
Came about her who holds now the key of the house.

GEORGE MACKAY BROWN

TWO WOMEN

Two women meet each morning to pray
One is a mother, the other her daughter
They belong to different religions
Only blood binds them together

Stephen is the object of their prayer
He is the grandson of one, the son of the other
He lives abroad
He does not want to come home
He wants to be left alone

So the women pray silently — each in her own way
Their words do not cross
They rise and converge
Stephen will be safe for another day.

NEVILLE BRAYBROOKE

ENGAGEMENT

windowpane frost morning
cold solitary waking
                knowing
        (yet still not knowing)
                you
thoughts awaking
earlyday still body
            hard comfort
            soft drifting
warmmoist memories of
fantasies of
                you

blinds drawn against chill evening
within together resting
                knowing
        (so soon now knowing)
                you
plans intertwining
daydrawn windrocked body
            hard truth
            soft dreaming
warmmoist fantasies of
memories of
                you

SUE ELKINS

WORDS OF CONSOLATION

When we have lost a loved one,
the one that is most dear,
And life itself seems empty,
Be sure that God is near.

For the garden in the winter,
That seems so cold and dead
Will surely come to life again,
For that is what God said.

Seedtime and harvest will not fail,
For I make all things new,
As I live again in the garden,
So I'll live again in you.

GEORGE WESTON

TWO

It's autumn holiday; the morning light
throws yellow spangles from the marmalade
placed, with rolls, for the breakfast we'll eat late.
The table has two views, and I have laid
the plates so that we each can look ahead
across the other's line of sight to sky
and trees, in squares, which we have claimed
as favourites. My choice is east; there lies
a windswept garden, where pale birches sigh,
shrug off their leaves and scatter them like crumbs.
In yours, dark firs protect a gorse which tries
to show more flowers before the winter comes.
I know that, whilst we eat, I'll turn to gaze
through your window; to understand your place.

ROSEMARY A. HECTOR

THE LOVER

When blazing sunset glory paints the sky,
And colour, light and fire inflame the eye.
     The Christ is courting
     Courting of his love.

When joyful dawn-winged birds on summer days
With sweetest music chant their Maker's praise,
     The Christ with singing
     Serenades his love.

When whispering wanton winds caress the trees
With silk-soft susurrations in the leaves,
     The Christ is calling,
     Calling to his love.

When water waves and plays and spumes and foams,
And falls in lace-like tumbles down smooth stones,
     The Christ is dancing,
     Dancing for his love.

When storm-gales howl and thunder tears the air,
And trembling, Earth herself seems in despair,
     The Christ is mourning,
     Mourning for his love.

When rain to rainbow turns at touch of sun,
And leaf and web with diamonds bright are hung,
     The Christ is weeping,
     Weeping for his love.

When all is shrouded in such still, chill snow
That none believes spring's joy again will grow,
      The Christ is waiting,
      Waiting for his love.

In all he made, the Christ is come to woo,
Beseeching, yearning, weak with love for you.
      Oh, Man! Will you not hear?
      You are his love.

SANDY CONWAY

A DOOR

— If it wasn't for me, what would you be?
— A twisted twig on a dying tree.

— If it wasn't for me, what would you have done?
— Howled on the ground and sucked my thumb.

— If it wasn't for me, what would you have seen?
— Drugs and thugs and hideous obscene.

— If it wasn't for me, what would you have known?
— Cruel minds, hard hearts, and a terrible throne.

— And who do you say that I am?
— You are my Lord, disguised as a dragon
— You are my Lord, disguised as a thief
— You are my Lord, disguised as murder
— You are my Lord, disguised as grief

— And what do you call your loss?
— Justice.
— And what do you call your suffering?
— Fire.
— And what do you call your emptiness?
— Door. A door. A door.

ALAN JACKSON

'IT WILL BE A RIVER . . . '

It will be a river
my small voice in you
which now trails weakly like a
stream among boulders

it will burn bright
the light which glows so strong,
so long, then flickers
wildly, blows unsteadily.

Clowns now, you will be dancers
at my throne. Do you not see it,
all fears gone
you will wear glory like a gown.

For now be foolish, clumsy,
stumble, fall.
All shall be well
and being unwhole is part of travelling.

Let me hear your heart sing
be my clown
and it will be a river
my small truth in you.

JILL HARRIS

SPASTICS

Chair, brace, straps,
steel, wheel,
mould, sponge support;
machinery of a sort;
hard, unyielding armour
lest folded in its languor
the body should collapse.

Tiny limpid creature
encased within a shell
clutching, crooked hand
attempts to tell
us that you understand—
with blissboard or gadget
fingers grope, fidget,
shrunk arms gesture.

But roll up for the ceilidh!
Strike up the tune!
in rhythm and music
to all else immune:
no longer spastic
bound to a wheelchair
body beyond repair,
but soul of life's party.

Distorted in frame
blessed are ye poor
irrecoverably happy
from hour to hour:
your shrieks of ecstasy
almost I weep to see
such leaping lame!

TESSA RANSFORD

PRESENCE

God speaks to me in silence,
The blackbird, hopping on the lawn;
The sunshine, the sea and the white sails.
The sea-gulls, resting on the old sea wall.

God speaks to me in laughter,
In the smiles of children at play:
In the caring eyes of a mother
As she teaches her child to pray.

God speaks to me in music,
In the crystal clear notes on the flute:
In the delicate air of a symphony,
Revealing the Presence of God.

SISTER MARGARET

IN THE CHAPEL AT DORNIE, WESTER ROSS

The place is set for a small Eucharist
in the chapel still smelling of newness.
Under its roof of compressed straw
a congregation is gathered,
visitors from Glasgow and the south.

To start the service, ritual prescribes
the choosing of the hymns
the preparation of the altar, adorning
oneself in eucharistic vestments,
the lighting of candles. Which is why,
in the stillness of the cloud driven
morning, eyes fixed on the back of my neck,
I struggle to strike the damp, highland
matches on the soft box,
before the word can be spoken or the bread broken.

GEOFFREY SMITH

THE PRAYER STOOL

I leave aside my shoes
        — my ambitions,
undo my watch
        — my timetable,
take off my glasses
        — my views,
unclip my pen
        — my work,
put down my keys
        — my security,
to be alone with You,
  the only true God.

  After being with You,
I take up my shoes
  to talk in Your ways,
strap on my watch
  to live in Your time,
put on my glasses
  to look at Your world,
clip on my pen
  to write up Your thoughts,
pick up my keys
  to open Your doors.

GRAHAM KINGS

LETTER FROM ASSISI

Francis to his Father
Father, if only you had understood
I craved to be the man of every hour –
All your ambition slept deep in my blood.

I loved the feel of silk, the touch of power,
To gossip, joke, outshine Assisi's cavaliers;
For all the talk of bird or flower

I had your merchant's will to vie. Two years
Caught a prisoner in Perugia, I was still
Half-aware I'd fought for a town's profiteers.

A ransom – than the homecoming. 'Is Francis ill
Or in love?' people asked, wondered why
I looked so distant; I did the parties until

Something snapped. Every stricken passer-by
Now fixed his stare on me, saying 'Francis,
All turns on you; Francis, look in my eye!'

There were riches in Apulia – I had lances,
Troubadour's songs to sing. I could forget.
But haunted daily by those strangers' glances,

I sold your bale of scarlet cloth to let
Some paupers feed. Father, you whipped me,
Branded me a madman; each time we met

You cursed, so I paid a down-and-out his fee
To bless me as a father, taunt your sorrow —
For I would outdo, best the world in poverty.

I was young and life tomorrow.
Already my followers scheme for a benefice;
The road seemed short — I could beg or borrow

Rags of humility, call your care avarice.
Time unlocks compassion's garden-gate;
Father, I bid you forgive my Judas kiss.

MICHEAL O'SIADHAIL

PRAYER

Romans 8:26–28

Desires all fall away when you are near,
Except the one, which is to be with you.
The heart is filled with love which casts out fear
And there is only one thing left to do:
Utter the single sound the soul can make,
Filled to the brim with what it can't contain,
Opening blinded eyes made clear awake,
And tasting sweetness after so much pain.

Power that brings the soul into your care,
Moved on the waters, moves now in the heart,
And now there's nothing else for me but prayer
Not knowing what to say, but keen to start
By praying prayer that I cannot express,
By coming to you in my nothingness.

NEIL PERRY

PRAYER

To be a stream in haste to join the ocean wide,
Lost within its depths. Evaporating then,
To fall as rain — refreshed, refreshing, clean.

To be a grain of sand, washed over by the tide,
Lost upon the shore. And then becoming firm,
The surface where God's footprints may be seen.

To be a note of music, pure melodic sound,
Lost in symphony. And then be played to blend
in harmony with orchestra divine.

To be a drop of glass, the Craftsman's rod wrapped round,
Lost within the fire. Then purified and shaped
Into the goblet for the heavenly wine.

To lose awareness, yet become the more aware —
This . . . this is prayer.

M.J. NORMAN

ORTHODOX LITURGY

Here in a holy dimness filled with angels, like the cave
Of Christ's Nativity, starred with the lamps' red fire,
The dome a bowl of incense, where the Pantocrator
Blesses and judges, deep voices strongly yearn to God;
Holy our God, holy and strong, holy and immortal
Have mercy on us. Blanched flames of candles flicker
Before the icons; the Theotokos holds up her Son;
The Holy Fathers bow down before Him whose nature they defined;
The Ascetics fast for the banquet of the Messiah;
The faithful of flesh and fresco are consanguineous —
We who still wage the warfare know that these have not forgotten;
At their supplication, O God, visit, have mercy on us
Behind the Royal Doors the Spirit comes; now bread and wine
Are made for holy ones the Holy Things, pledges of life;
Now we have seen the true Light; we worship the Trinity
Their bodies are bending and rising like wind-tossed grain;
Fingers trace in air the sign of death-struck-dead;
Imperial Byzantium lives still in these gestures —
Cultic movements, fitting courtiers of the Basileus.
This rustic whitewashed chapel is now 'the Holy Wisdom'
Resplendent with the mystic commerce of the royal feast;
'We stood bewildered, not aware if this was earth or heaven
But recognize that God has made his dwelling here with man.'[1]
The priest dismisses us under the blessing and mercy —
From the edge of eternity we sink back into time;
Into the breathless brazen light and sharp-edged shadows of day —
That light which mystics see is but the shadow of God;
Until we came here we did not know we had been exiles
But entering this unknown church we find we have come home.

TERENCE TOWERS

[1] *Ambassadors of the still pagan Vladmir, Prince of Kiev, attended a service*
in the Church of the Holy Wisdom, Ayia Sophia, in Constantinople, and
reported back to their master in these words

'O GOD! YOU FORD THE SILENCE . . . '

O God! You ford the silence of the night,
when all is dark, and yet the soul is light,
when quietness stills the spirit, sets us free,
and blackness leads us to eternity.

Tonight I spurn the sluggish ways of sleep,
and know the God who spins the starry deep,
the trees talk night, the cross is chaste and cool,
and gentle stillness is our rod and rule.

RAYNE MACKINNON

WAY
OF THE CROSS

'PUT A NAME . . . '

Put a name to my sorrows
and I shall let them pass
loose my angry grip upon
these precious shards of glass

but the name must be grand and great
the name must be true
spoken on a hill's side
cold in the dew

O I see the name printed
printed on the page
and tears come running in a stream
releasing my rage

I let go the fragments
my palm begins to bleed
the name of my sorrows
who climbs a hill may read

VERONICA ZUNDEL

THE FIRE

It was not life that drew him from the flames,
but rescuers who pulled him safely out.
His friend was trapped beyond their help, the boy
he'd known through years of jeopardy and joy,
how could he leave him, who had shared those shifts
of youth? He plunged back to him with a shout,
thus reaching, like the unreturning dove,
a fiery landfall, that would set him free.
Did love reject all life's unopened gifts,
preferring what was known to what might be?
Oh no, it was the truth of childhood's games.
He left the deadly body, fired by love,
that ghostly flame, whose nature he would learn
though quickly his most willing flesh must burn.

JOHN BATE

*This poem was written in memory of a young boy who, rescued from a fire,
returned to the burning house to try to save his friend – and died in
the attempt.*

A LETTER FROM KIEV

. . . The autumn rains came just as the ground on which the foundation for the stadium was to be set had been dug out and loosened. A landslide . . . poured down on to the heavily populated . . . Podol. . . .
Refusenik Mark Ya Azbel

Rochele, dearest child, this letter comes
from me, mired so long in an old sorrow,
to you, in your new life, your happy country.

I think of you often, see the fields of grain
from sky to sky, your house a small island,

and would have come by now, to make a life,
feed hens, scour pans, and watch the children grow,

but stayed, to look each evening towards the height
of Babi Yar, where Hannah and Moishele died,
where their small bones lie.

                    But listen, Rochele —
do you remember how we angered them? —
old women, obstinate, toiling upwards, short
of breath, stubborn of memory, bringing
stones of remembrance in our fists. They tired
of turning us back. 'This is not a place to weep,'
they said. 'We will make it a place to dance.'

I tell you no lie, Rochele. They said so.
A stadium, they said, and a dancing floor.

And so they brought the great machines, to gouge
the hillside out, and then the autumn rains
came down like Noah's flood, and churned that ground
into a heaving tide of mud that rolled
down — and the bones, Rochele, the bones
that saw the light again, thighbones, fingers,
skulls — turning over and over, rolling
down on the crowded Podol, shops and streets
and trams, smothering all in thick silence.

I tell you, Rochele, God is not sleeping.
He would not let them dance above our dead.

Send me the ticket, Rochele. I am coming.

EVANGELINE PATERSON

EXILES

Behind net curtains windows fogged and streamed,
Trams sparkled like flints, the cobbles echoed frost;
They sat as if in Moscow, hunched and pale
Like winter palaces awaiting snow.

Whole lives had been spent waiting for the knocks
Of men in greatcoats, vehicles with drawn blinds
Waiting outside; for coded, furtive taps
From those evading lamps or coming back
Into small rooms after the huge white cold,
Of signals for the visitors to leave.

The samovar was full, dumplings prepared,
They always served some goulash after nine;
A candle fluttered and the icon flinched
Until the sound of footsteps died away.

MARTYN HALSALL

JUNGLE BRIDGE-BUILDER

In Thailand's
muddy jungle, with the
monsoon-swept river,
flooding down to the sea.
Tides of brown water
bearing broken trees
and drowned cattle
and cholera bacilli.
Some of us were building
wooden bridges, to take
the railway line to Burma.
You were making every day
bridges of words
between us and our enemy.
Essential equipment for you,
not pick or shovel, nor
dynamite and drill, but
two fat dictionaries and
years of labour with the
language in Japan.

These delicate lines of communication
were liable to be swept away by
storms of anger, explosive rages and
small, insidious suspicions.
Such frail bridges broken
could mean violent blows,
beatings, hate-generated cunning,
even death for some.
But you who knew the enemy best
saw their human hearts,
prayed in public for their
welfare, and by this action
set some of us on the everlasting
way to the Peaceful Kingdom.
'How blest are the peacemakers:
God shall call them his sons.'

W.H. ALLCHIN

NOT AN ASSAULT

A white police reservist was acquitted of assault after flogging a black woman with a rhino whip in Zimbabwe, Rhodesia: 'The exigencies of the situation demanded it.'

She was alone, you see;
There we were, on patrol, expecting to find guerillas;
Men with guns, menacing whites, able to defend themselves,
And kill us. I led the patrol. I could not lose face again
By missing black faces hidden in the dark.
She must have known where they were;
She made me so mad, pretending she knew nothing.
It was imperative I flog her, to make her speak.
Oh, yes she screamed all right but no words.
You know the rhino whip tears the flesh right to the bone.
Great ribbons of flesh, black skin,
Red blood and screaming, screaming.
They can't stand the pain, you see.
What's that? Oh, no, she didn't speak.
I had to keep on and on, the sweat came to my hands,
My mouth tasted salt as I watched
The thickened leather of the rhino hide
Tear her gradually to broken pulp.
It was necessary to get the truth, to find
Their hiding black faces, it was their fault, not mine.
If they had been there they would have fought us,
Perhaps injured us or even killed;
We had to beat her, the exigencies of the situation
                                        demanded it.
The jury never asked why I had whip and gun.
What was that? No we never found a trace of them.
She never spoke you see. Damn her, we don't even know
If they were there.

JOAN BROCKELSBY

STUTTGART STAATSGALLERIE
SEPTEMBER 1987

Following a guided tour of the Stirling gallery, in which we were led to five modern works of art. Three are described here.

This black screen through which no light shines
yet has a form, the guide insists,
don't guess its aim, but study the lines
— a square without direction, now observe it near,
other colours are hidden there and if you persist
you will see painted squares and a cross appear
standing behind the gloom.

The next feels equally dense and dark,
without a shape. The guide explains:
follow each arc, each mark
a history of pots hung from a string
and sense the swing, here slow, there fast, the rains
washing away old forms of surface display,
fashioning a new work.

That scarred wood, old rope and nails,
is known without the painted cross in red.
But there is more to understand, the guide enthused:
The shining needle, Jesus hanging on a thread,
symbolizes pain; the bottles, Mary and John,
were full of pills too often used.
If now undrugged you feel reality
as hurt, learn that needle and thread's activity
can also heal.

DAVID PULLINGER

TRUTH-SIGN

My name is Truth-sign
it was not given by a priest
it was given by God who loves truth-tellers
of whom I am least

Out of the mouths of infants
shall truth come
it is too long, the child cried
I have been dumb

She began to tell the truth
as true as she could
she heard the nails driven through
flesh, bone, wood

She felt the cold iron
enter her soul
it was when her flesh most was torn
she knew herself whole

Truth-sign is my name, she cried
name me no other
you are not my father
you are not my mother

I have but one father
neither preacher nor priest
the father of truth-tellers
of whom I am least

VERONICA ZUNDEL

KERNELS OF CORN

Yeshua came running, breathlessly running
     home from his play,
  watching his homecoming
  dove, restlessly swinging
  his basket and spilling
  kernels of corn on the way.

And a forest of crosses, that unwilling
nightmare whirled in his brain on his way.

'Forget all those crosses, son, and the pain
     you saw that day.
Each year the sower scatters his grain;
each year the harvest ripens again.
This is old wisdom, learn it and gain
peace. We've all got to die some day.'

'Not publicly, mother, stretched
     choking that way?'
'Forget it,' she urged, but she stitched
thoughts which pricked as she patched
her cloth. 'Be careful,' she thought, 'or I'll catch
     myself telling him of the day

when the angel came, of those words which
     will pierce my own heart one day.'

JENNY ROBERTSON

THE HOUSE

Into such solid rock
How shall a house be built? Let them see to it.

After the rains men dug to the hard rock.
The carpenter strove with the roof-tree.

A scaffolding fell.
Three drunk labourers were given their books.

She who was to grace the finished house,
Baker of loaves, keeper of the loom,
She stood in a web of rafters.

The work languished. Another mason was sent for,
A man of solid reputation.

One hot day a girl took a jar of ale to the site.

Thunder in August wrenched an iron lattice,
A sudden brilliance out of the banked grey and purple.

Masons laid a lintel, a long cold stone.

Women stood here and there.
They gossipped. They nodded. They said, 'house of sorrow'.

Before harvest; labourers climbed down from the eaves.

A diviner went in a slow dance.
Earth was struck into tumults of bright circles.

Dazzle, first snow on planed and sanded pine.

At the time of crocuses
Carpenters put the last nail in the staircase.

Painters, tilers, men with snibs and latches —
Ladders and planks and buckets borne away.
The architect's voice from the balcony, 'It is finished.'

The woman came again with daffodils.
She set a jar on the sill.

And still the house echoed like a tomb
Till the village women arrived with gifts.
They stayed to eat the cakes from the new-lit hearth.

GEORGE MACKAY BROWN

JOSEPH

Call me
>Bar Jacob, bar David,
>Known to Nazarenes, few else,
>Carver of the olive.

Shaper
>Of the plough, bowl and bed
>Table, plate, chair and spoon,
>Bound to the Lord, his Son,
>And my Mary in love.

His, hers
>And mine, the aching pain
>Of the cross, so slowly dragged
>Past Romans, Pharisees,
>Who could not understand

That I
>Worker of the hard wood
>Was also moulded, chiselled
>To something beautiful,
>Carved by the Lord.

AIDAN DOHERTY

TRIDUUM

Feria v in Coena Domine

He who has riches now must come to dwell
in the lean parish of hunger, there to learn
that blessedness is not to buy and sell
that what we get is seldom what we earn.
Before the bread is broken, wine is poured
he must make payment he can ill afford.

And they must come who crown or mitre wear
to do the Maundy and to bend the knee;
for words come cheap but actions cost us dear
and they must make their peace with poverty.
Before the bread is broken, wine is poured
we say the grace, but grace speaks its own word.

He who is blind to want or grief must pray
some gracious touch to open now his eyes;
that his afflicted Saviour he may
in stranger or in brother recognize.
Then bread is broken and the wine is poured,
This is the Pasch the supper of the Lord.

Feria vi in Passione et Morte Domini

Faithful Cross sustain your burden
do not splinter, do not crack,
though the load of all our sorrows
hangs, a deadweight, on your back.
Upright on the hill of sadness
in the gale of evil's power,
hold him strongly, hold him gently
at his covenanted hour.

Matchless in the forest mounting
shoot and sapling, branch and tree;
felled, dismembered, planed and jointed,
for this day's dark mystery.
Gibbet, infamous, ennobled
by this death and by this birth
hold your cross-grained branches open
harbour for a ship-wrecked earth.

When, the noon-tide darkness ended,
he whom you have borne is dead,
in his mother's arms laid softly,
you are left untenanted;
sharp against the soul's horizon
still uphold us, shining tree,
emblem of the Saviour's passion
standard of his victory.

KEVIN NICHOLS

LAST SUPPER

There is a point and that point only
where all skew passions meet and lull;
as wave takes pause against the shore
my heart in this heart finds its core
where bread and wine are breakfast truly
and make the lean heart full.

For hungry hearts are near to choose
and hungrier for seeking;
but heart to heart makes scanty feast:
the lesser cannot raise the least
nor ravaged be renewed with use
nor broken mend by breaking.

Yet here such wry distinctions end
and living ways to death that tend,
here, at this death made living;
never food filled the starving dead
until this wine, until this bread,
crux where all raging questions blend
laid rest in this forgiving.

VERONICA ZUNDEL

GOLGOTHA

The stars weep salt tears over Earth's unrest,
And women weep for men with their own hard,
Hungry heroics; Earth is all around,
And Earth is old.
But Heaven is eternally fresh and young,
And rounds the Earth's false age with women's tears —
'Ye daughters of Jerusalem, weep.'
On Golgotha a heavy afternoon
Was dull and stubborn, when the Lord of All.
Cursed by Caiaphas, heard the hard hiss
Of serpent tongues that jeered at Man and God.
The officers, confused and humble men
Merely fulfilled their task; the soldiers played
At dice beneath the cross, that, huge and high,
Is hanging over all the Earth.
And there Christ heard the jeers and sneers
Of intellectuals and the passers-by,
Only intent on their own cleverness,
Who jested over Mankind's agony,
When all of Heaven was deserted, dead
To Jesus' cry:
'My God, My God, why hast Thou forsaken me?'

We have betrayed the Lord, each one of us,
Who have lost God, though only for a while,
Have heard the cry of despair and utter loss.
Earth teetered then on tragedy, and Heaven
Was suffering with one man. The women still
Wept tears, and these washed clean the clotted gore,
The drops of sweat, shed in Gethsemane.
Now darkness deepened, and at the ninth hour
Death rattled, twisted in the Saviour's throat —
'All is fulfilled.'

Then mankind's curse on Christ
Was buried with the Saviour in the tomb.
Two days went by, and still the women wept,
Washed clean, the blood, the bitterness; washed clean
The earth, the rock, the tomb.
Their tears flowed ever downward to the ground,
Reached to the roots of flowers, and now all spring
Was resurrected, when the rock rolled back,
The angels present. Then a woman spoke
To Jesus in the garden's spread and shade,
And at a woman's voice,
The followers of Jesus, cowards all,
Came running to the purged and empty tomb.

RAYNE MACKINNON

RESURRECTION

EASTER SATURDAY
OR 'HAS ANYONE HERE SEEN THOMAS?'

Sometimes I feel
like an Easter Saturday,
               just
a tombful of possibilities
wishing my guard
would fall asleep.

GODFREY RUST

THANKSGIVING

We give thanks for St Thomas
  All we who have known
  The darkness of disbelief,
The hollowness at the heart of Christmas,
The intolerable emptiness of Easter,
  The grief of separation.

With Thy great mercy Thou dost enfold us,
The waverers, the aliens, who stood apart, alone.
  For the impoverishment of our barren years
    Thou wilt atone.

Now with the faithful company we bring,
From depths of thankfulness
    Our adoration
     To Thee,
    O, Christ our King.

EDITH FORREST

SEQUENCES

Words fetched to furnish the great soaring
basilicas of the Gregorian tropes;
as we pace with words the heart's inarticulate
cadenzas, its long sadness and its hope.

Its long sadness and its hope moulded
by syllables, begins to write itself
into new stanzas and to make new sense,
to soothe and celebrate, falling into the movement
of your metre, Lord Christ, and of your cadence.

Of your cadence Adonai, from the Empyrean,
your bright and dazzling Advent here eclipsed
in the mists of middle earth and of your journey
through the bazaars of our strange condition,
sore-footed, making towards the sad mountain.

The sad mountain where in a gale of grief,
cut by scourge and lance to the quick of the heart
you weathered for us the dark storm of tears,
tears for the things of men and for their follies
unshed, unsaid in our dumb heart's blocked fountain.

Fountain of fire, springing on the third morning
from the dim cave of flickering lights and shadows
from the sepulchre surging into the sunlight;
soar Lord of life, and in your crescendo
be our zenith, O be our meridian.

KEVIN NICHOLS

NOLI ME TANGERE

But I would not had he not forbade it,
For he had about him something awesome;
Familiar? Yes, for I had called his name
And he had beckoned me, but also strange;
I who had often bathed his feet,
Could no more touch him than I could a flame;

And flame he seemed to be.

My downward gaze saw his hands,
his feet, his side,
But I felt no pity for his wounds,
For he bore them as a victor
Bears his trophies home.
I raised my head and saw, on his face
A glory that transformed this place
Of tombs. The dawn that glimmered in the east
Seemed shadow to his light,
The olives seemed to sing his name.
Blessing and blessed that hour of meeting was
Was, and is now and is eternity,
For when I die I shall meet him as we met
But then he will take me by the hand,
For I may touch him in his timeless land.

STANLEY COOKE

MATRIOSHKA FOR JOANNA AND MARY

These curvy, passive ladies
with painted smirks,
flat featured, which uncup
to hold identicals.
Why do they seem appropriate
as an Easter gift?
Easter, when women
(limbs spiked with shock,
triumphant arms, ankles
turned to dance), ran
breathless with first news?
It is their emptiness,
filled only with another
and another birth.
Wood turned like eggshell
reminds. Each generation
opens up, tells news
identical.

ROSEMARY A. HECTOR

EASTER HYMN

When all is dark and doubt and dim
I only know I think of him
Who died to set the sinner free,
Jesus my God who died for me,
Who bore the jeers, the taunts, the scorns,
The kisses and the crown of thorns.

When your disciples fled away
You rose again at break of day.
When all had been death, doubt and gloom,
Mary came to the evening tomb —
The angels kept their watch and guard,
The gates of hell were then unbarred.

And now you rise at break of day.
Be with us now, dear Lord, we pray.
Be with us now through all the world.
Set all the flags of heaven uncurled.
Be with us all through this dear clime,
Be with us till the end of time.

RAYNE MACKINNON

RESURRECTION

The year now floats in an eternal calm,
Buttressed on fragile rafts of leafy green,
And winds, now tamed, ate licking at the grass
Like friendly dogs. Three months back, the world rose,
As it will always rise,
And toothless winter muttered to itself
In senile impotence. The season though,
Merely redoubles, echoes and reflects
Eternal resurrection. Once I saw
Christ rise and shine
In the old woman in her withered coat
Who fed the pigeons: one by one they perched
Upon the seat, upon her lap, their wings
Agog with greed; she'd shoo them off, then scoop
Out yet more chunks of bread from an old bag,
And when a squirrel bounced across the path,
Held up two pleading paws, she'd always throw
Some peanuts in his way.

There's kindliness
Alive in the most bitter heart, all sour
With spleen. The coarsest tongue can brighten, bless
Man's hopelessness. Christ, like a spring, is risen,
Divides into a thousand streams, that thread
Their way thru all life's dirt, and pluck the stains
Off weary souls.
Listen! A dog is barking, and the gull's
White feathers, clearer than the clouds, were made
To match the miracle of flight; the day
Is dull, it seems, but forget-me-nots,
Each tiny, fragile petal all alive,
Breathe sweetness on the soil.
And when in the dull throb of death, the soul
sings clearer, then eternity will watch
With patient eyes, and the low lamps of life
will feel a brighter light
Shine thru Man's weakness and his ignorance.

RAYNE MACKINNON

GILDED SPLINTERS

as eggshells
              underfoot

but, tread carefully!
not ours to shatter
the new-laid path.
half-blind we walk
in pre-dawn dark,
fragile and broken
we trample fragility.

but, look carefully!
the rising sun is golden;
and where we've journeyed
shattered shells disclose
new life; the wind
is at our backs
to urge us on,

now seeing.
behind, searing shards
scatter light;
ahead, reflections: clear
gold of zenith gold.
but follow carefully
the footsteps of the guide.

and
who am i
to let scarlet flooding
pains from gilded splinters
hold me back?
the feet that go before
are nail-pierced.

SUE ELKINS

EVIDENCE OF THE RESURRECTION
TO TAKE HOME WITH YOU

After He'd gone
the breakfast was like a dream.
Did we really smell the
smoke spindling into
pale blue dawn
watch the lake's waves
lap at the sand
cook fresh caught fish ˙
on the fire
eat bread
and He
here among us?

Hot afternoon
tracing footsteps in sand
finding the circle of sticks
charcoal dust
grainy on shells
bread crumbs
and here in your fingers
the white needle bones
of the fish
which He
really ate.

ELIZABETH BURNS

MERCY IN OUR TIME

Let not mistaken mercy
blind my fading sight,
no false euphoria lull me.
I would not unprepared
take this last journey.
Give me a light to guide me
through dark valleys,
a staff to lean upon,
bread to sustain me,
a blessing in my ear
that fear may not assail me.
Then leaving do not hold my hand,
I go to meet a friend —
    that same who traced
   compassion in the sand.

NANCY HOPKINS

INSIGHT

Here on the altar, here lies the bread,
Jesus my Saviour is living, not dead.

Eyes of the body see but the bread,
Eyes of the spirit see the Godhead.

AN UNKNOWN SCHOOLBOY

CORN KING

Corn King
      spring!
leap, leap. Lord of light,
dance, dance, dear delight.

Grain buried deep
today, tomorrow, sleep
      then
      lightward
      larkward
      skyward
      Godward
          leap
      bright to death

Broken corn King harvested,
thrashed, ground, milled for bread
      at daylight leap
      from your dark sleep.

Harvester, begin
the dance, the dear delight.
Yielded sheaves, golden bright,
      a garnered horde
welcome their harvest lord
while corn-fat valleys shout and sing
      honouring
the harvest king,
      feasting
the harvest home
with broken bread and one cry: *Come!*

JENNY ROBERTSON

A
TOUCH OF
FLAME

THE JEWEL

We hurried out to look at the sun
Solemn and fierce in the west
Molten through slats of gold.
Our faces were washed with light
From that bright confessional.
But we knew we were prisoners, longing,
Calling out for the free gift of life.

Ideas of colour change
With apple, lilac and rose
And the royal gold intense
Far-flung and careless as kings' bounty,
How long is a moment awash with joy?
We hopped like a child from foot to foot
Till at last it all capsized and sank.

Even then the treasure was yet to come
For in the blackness of the trees
Rose turned to ruby red as embers,
The precious stone answering blood
Flesh of our flesh and secret of bone.
Was it a fresh start, not an ending?

SISTER MARY LAURENCE

PAPHOS, CYPRUS

In the still
afternoon
a cock crowed
senselessly:
the sun shone on.
There when the Roman
city's columns stood
a taunted Paul
proclaimed
his living Christ.

Long since
earthquake on earthquake
tumbled all
and left deserted:
but the churches spread
and the witness
of that convert
rumbles on
forever
round the world.

CHARLES LOVELL

RUBLEV'S ICON

Atheists guard the angels:
the Soviets treasure
that trinity of beings
Abraham addressed as 'Lord';
amid primitive violence
the man who painted them
tried to live a pure life,
Their tranquility contains
excess; the people blow
kisses at the plate glass.
Guards, guarded and angels
make another trinity.

JOHN BATE

The Holy Trinity, *by Andrei Rublev is perhaps the best known and best loved of all Russian icons. It hangs now in the Tetriakov Gallery in Moscow.*

DARK NIGHT OF THE SPIRIT

Swords rust in attics
regarded antiquated
non-conducive to material satisfaction.

Mental fight requires the word-in-hand
that sleeps not in its sheath
but wreaks a spiritual havoc:

A havoc like the hurricane of spirit
Geist — full of rampant gusts
to blow us wildly off the beaten track.

The flame that lights our life
is spluttering for lack of oxygen:
inspiration comes in frantic gasps.

      *   *   *

Dark, mature, wise woman,
hidden part of god, revealed
to those alone who love her;

No emaciated professional 'ghost',
no father, son or virgin,
but *sophia*, black but comely.

Her favours will bring no high position
but parched, endless torment,
branded a troubadour.

Our song will be made welcome,
but we will be cast out
from the castles of this world.

Our lady must disown us all the more
whom she will meet in secret.
Choose power then, or wisdom!

      *   *   *

By night, O Nicodemus, you shall learn
of birth from god-the-Mother
if you watch while others sleep.

Nor put aside the sop she offers
bitter though it taste, sharp as betrayal:
the ultimate surrender: to be born.

Reward her ceaseless labour,
her great travail d'amour
to bring you where you may begin to breathe.

Reward her with your never-failing love,
your service in her cause,
your chariot racing through the realms of light.

She is the oxygen and you the flame;
she, the gale with tongues of fire
destroying our established habitations.

*   *   *

Run riot, *ruach*, through all the world!
Let darkness cover us!
Our tombs will be deserted then at dawn.

TESSA RANSFORD

ST JOHN OF THE CROSS, AT UBEDA

'As natural fire will burn
consuming in its turn
each object it may touch,
Your love indeed is such
a fire, within the heart
consuming every part,

if only we reach out
beyond distress and doubt,
and past the soul's dark night
will let that flame ignite
within ourselves to prove
the living flame of Love.

The prophet Jeremiah
aptly described this fire
as "hidden in his bones";
as we may know; it owns
body, mind, reason, will.
And yet — we tremble still,

so unfamiliar is
this total burning bliss;
You therefore temper it
to understanding fit,
cool every anguished burn
and let the soul return

to the serene repose
the accepted lover knows;
Love, I can scarce await
that final rapturous state,
but would experience
Your white-hot influence —

flame which my longing fans
"ignis existuans",
body, mind, soul of me
purify utterly;
naught would content my mind
more, than that purge to find!

So let your flame set free
from passion, fantasy,
me their conformist slave,
as a free son now save
from this destructive pride;
scorch me, to reach your side!'

H.O. BRIAN O'NEILL

PENTECOST

On an edge of seeing
vision split
through the leaves of stone
I slip and am lost . . .

the leaves sway my body
they rock and caress

the wind is my cradle
its spirit within

my head in the stars
deep rooted my heart

I weep in the night
and my tears are new born

I see from within
in my heart lies the fire

new growth in my sight
for tomorrow renewed

I awake to the Light
and the fire of thy Love

FRANCESCA GREENE

TREE OF GLORY

Malus Eleyi (purple flowering crab) in a year of abundance

This is the day of the full blossoming
of my purple fire-tree; all day long
I have felt the surge of ecstasy and power,
and now, in this May evening, in a mystic sky
of rose twilight, cascades of glory burst
from arching boughs — a silent Vesuvius —
the dark stem-cone erupting fragrant fire,
roots tapping treasure from earth's deep well.
The night glow lures me from my bed,
stealing my sight, as, with the setting sun
it burns to blood.

Never a year has the beacon failed —
its flame bringing beauty-worshippers,
strangers, to my door, to ask its name;
toil laid down and care dissolved in homage.
Brief glory before death, when blossoms pale,
strewing grey petal-ash thick as snow
for funeral token. Blossom-bereft, quiescent,
it will stand unremarkable, unremarked,
maturing slowly through summer
cherry-apples to cheer the winter boughs
and nourish woodland birds.

Now, for this burning hour of bloom,
is God's immortal glory glimpsed in mortal tree
— Creator in created, Christ flowering,
royal Christ in fragile blossom;
purple of kingship, pall and Passion;
blood of Christ, shed for many and for me;
redemption ransom; judgement fire, burning dross.
In this perfection is the end and the beginning,
death — and life eternal:
flower-fall yielding the promised fruit
of everlasting hope.

JOAN ROWBOTTOM

OLD CHESTNUT

Unfathomable grace, grace upon grace
that the same chestnut which surprised our childhood
in May with such munificence of flame
should punctually expend, year after year
its prodigal whiteness to delight our children
and teach them beauty.

More, that its bursting shells, the oldest joke
in nature, still after these many years
should scatter conkers down to satisfy
my sons and me and all October boys
one tree, all generations; grace upon grace
and of his fulness have all we received.

SIMON BAYNES

DANCE OF THE MONTHS

January comes with his ice-crown.
February spilling thaw and snowdrops.
March, bursting loud cheeks!
Then April, with a troop of lambs and daffodils.
May, keeper of peat-hill and cuithe-stream.
June, covering the night fire in the north.
July, tall and blue as lupins.
August with the cut cornstalks.
September, dusting cobwebs from the lamp.
October, good witch, with apples and nuts.
November, host to shades and hallows.
December, with snowflake and star.

In the inn of December, a fire.
A loaf, a bottle of wine.
Travellers, rich and poor, are on the roads.

GEORGE MACKAY BROWN

AN EXHIBITION OF ICONS

'Such colours'; 'such economy of line',
'How well that unknown artist trapped the light'
Coolly the cognoscenti praise and weigh
The merits of these squares of adze-smoothed wood
Which shine enamelled jewels in the rays
Of suns that set three hundred years ago.

The not-so-knowing read their catalogues
To place in context this exotic art
Where it was painted and perhaps for whom;
(Where is Pskov? Who was St Parasceve?)

Large-eyed, the icons gaze full face at us
Who gaze, with faint disquiet back at them —
Are we now judged, who came to see and judge?
Should we now rather reverence than admire?

These harmonies of colour, where the tints
Blend like the notes of music in a chord,
These imaged antitypes of holiness
Are not just 'art', but matter by man's mind
Made to articulate the praise of God.

Hung on these hessianed walls, hygienic, chic,
Spotlighted in controlled humidity
These are gagged icons, pinned-out specimens.
But in the context of the Liturgy
Backed by the crumbling whitewash of some church
Where doves nest in the dome, and candle-smoke
Blunts the bright colours, then the icons preach
Their sermons on the text of God-made-man,
And show the Christian hope, in picturing
The resurrection bodies of the saints —
Not paintings, but Creation made anew.

TERENCE TOWERS

ALLEGRI'S MISERERE IN KING'S COLLEGE CHAPEL, CAMBRIDGE

'The sacrifice of God is a troubled spirit:
a broken and contrite heart, O God, shalt thou not
despise.'

Boldly into an irridescent vault
the voices climb. Colours confuse their way
but still their yearning clears
for the white cry, the prism's mended joy.

Softened by harmonies of willed ascent
the roof, stone-forested, dissolves in cloud;
effortless beckoning depths
tempt them into octaves higher than sound.

Leaping, one voice treads air, almost upheld
then stills his fluttering cadences; his clear
cry gathers colour, sinks
grieving through the spectrum of the choir.

Again words ramify. High up, the roof
settles delicate boughs. Impenetrable
now is the way the child
found home that moment on one syllable.

Stained with rainbow discords, merged with doubt,
a hueless healing mends beyond belief.
And that joy sears again;
knife-bright and irreducible its grief.

JENNIFER DINES

LEARNING HEBREW

Wrestling with angels on the edge of dark
I strain to master this rough-muscled tongue,
to grasp its energetic ciphers, stark
with chemistry that's straight from chaos sprung.
Its structure programmed, each swart syllable
builds up its crystals, as from tight-packed seed
forests unfold. Majestic, voluble
with sounds whose carbons grow from silence freed
for speech at last, my seraph masters me.
I burn; I read the words creation spoke —
the prophecy of stars pointed in flame,
the chanted scrolls of dark and rhythmic sea,
the half-voiced gutturals of the thunder's throat —
and name it, the unutterable Name.

JENNIFER DINES

DANTE

The bitter winds that squeezed the air
soften from passion and from care
into a vision, cleaving rare.

Into a few warm souls there start
the sacred words that hush the heart,
words that can dim the mere world's mart.

And Dante too makes taut the vice
that holds the soul in Paradise
after he passed through death's realm twice.

Vision of heaven I'll never find
while I am here among mankind
for which my words are coarse and blind.

Yet I must make my language clear
to fit the fervour of the scene,
echo the angels' shine and sheen.

O words inspired that raise the soul,
when Dante sees all heaven whole
travels through spheres that rise and roll.

A few brief words are all I claim,
sink back into the low world's shame,
knowing my spirit lost and lame.

RAYNE MACKINNON

DEUS ABSCONDITUS

Content? Hardly that.
Not for me the images
Of satisfaction, feeding full upon
Green pastures, sweet waters.

Rather, a willed acceptance
Of how You chose to be:
The mystery hidden
Since before Time was,
Compelling our perusal;
The irresolvable tension
Betwixt knowing and unknowing,
Balancing in the awareness
That what our search requires
Must be Your presence, somewhere.

So Pascal got it right;
Hunger implies the bread,
And our questioning, Your existence.

JOY FRENCH

STILLPOINT

Join your hands gently;
Let the world be placed
Beyond their reach,
Beyond their itch
Always to be doing;
Exempt from speech
This little space thus formed
Between your folded fingers,
Between your going
And your slow return —
This still enclosure
With its own high walls:
Join your hands gently, so,
No lovelier way than this of letting go.

JEAN M. WATT

PRAYER

O God, my God, risen above,
when shall I know the grasp of love,
that binds the soul, casts it beyond
the world of oak, bracken and pond?
When shall I feel my spirit leap
Through the dull mists of sloth and sleep?

O living Lord who stirs the skies,
My grain of seed withers, dies,
shrivels in passion's angry heat,
but does not rise again as wheat.
When shall I know you truly mine?
When shall I drink the Kingdom's wine?

O, Spirit pure, I hear you call,
tame my tempest once for all,
say I wish my neighbour's good
more than I wish for clothing, food.
And may I praise you every day
along the clear, yet clouded way.

RAYNE MACKINNON

EARLY IRISH LYRIC

Once again picture him near St Gall,
A monk in exile. Cinctured, diligent,
He is glossing, paving a Latin grammar.

'There are persons in the noun and particle,
Though they are infinite!' He annotates the text
With his cryptic memory aids. Today's

Lesson prepared, he unbends, daydreams.
It is early morning. Suddenly fired,
High on the elixir of spring, he declares:

'A hedge of trees overlooks me; for me
A blackbird sings – news I won't conceal . . . '
Febrile, meticulous, he chronicled the astoundment

A thousand years ago on the lower edge
Of a vellum folio. This is another spring
And we are brothers conjugate in ecstasy.

Something ignites. Possessed by the flame
The psyche hums. On a jag of ink
A nib travels in delirium tremens.

MICHEAL O'SIADHAIL

ACKNOWLEDGMENTS

Thanks to Tessa Ransford of the Scottish Poetry Library and to members of the Fellowship of Christian Writers who helped me trace poets; also to the editors of *The Tablet*, *Church of England Newspaper*, *Church Times* and *Third Way* who allowed me to request readers to submit poetry.

All poems are copyright and appear by permission of their authors. Many have been published in books and magazines, including *The Tablet*, *The Month*, *Catholic Education Today*, *Orbis*, *Lines Review*, *Chapman*, *Christian Poetry*, *Science of Thought Review*, *Omega* (Australia), *Temenos* and *Chelmer Arts Festival*.

The following poems have been published in books, and permission to include them here has been given by the copyright holders.

John Bate, 'Visitation', 'Tears', 'The Fire', 'Rublev's Icon' from *Damaged Beauty Needs a New Design*, The Gamecock Press, reprinted by permission of the author.

Olive Fraser, 'Glen of the Clearances', from *The Pure Account*, Aberdeen University Press, reprinted by permission of the publisher.

Nancy Hopkins, 'Mercy in our Time', from *Symphony*, Bemerton Press, reprinted by permission of the author.

Alan Jackson, 'This Story', 'Conundrum', 'The Door', from *Heart of the Sun*, reprinted by permission of the author.

Rayne Mackinnon, 'Peace', 'Prayer', 'Let's just suppose . . . ', 'Golgotha', from *Northern Elegies*, Netherbow Arts Centre, reprinted by permission of the author.

William Neill, 'Celtic Chapel', 'Church History', 'Sermon from Mid-Lent Sunday', from *Wild Places*, Luath Press, reprinted by permission of publisher and author.

Tessa Ransford, 'April 16th', from *Shadows from the Greater Hill*, 'Dark Night of the Spirit', from *Fools and Angels*, Ramsay Head Press, reprinted by permission of the author.

Micheal O'Siadhail, 'Aubade', 'Early Irish Lyric', from *Springnight*, 'Letters from Assisi', 'For my Friends', 'Lunchtime in a London Cafe' from *The Image Wheel*, Bluett and Company, reprinted by permission of the author.

BIOGRAPHICAL NOTES

DR WILLIAM ALLCHIN lives in Winchester, Hampshire. An almost life-long Christian, he is actively concerned in Peacemaking. He works as a psychotherapist, writer and WEA tutor.

DAVID BARRATT lectures in English at Chester College, one of his interests being Children's Literature. His book C.S. *Lewis and his World* was published recently; he also writes on aspects of faith and literature. He and his wife, Janet, have travelled widely and have lived in Pakistan and the USA.

JOHN BATE Author of several long narrative poems, including presentations of the lives of Florence Nightingale, Margaret Clitherow and Gwen John, and a book of lyrics, *Damaged Beauty Needs a New Design*, from which the poems published here are taken. He has also written various poetry brochures, such as *Tablet-ed*. A native of Cornwall, he now lives in Oxford.

NEVILLE BAYBROOKE has published poems in *The New Statesman*, *The Spectator* and *The Tablet*.

SIMON BAYNES Vicar of Winkfield, Windsor, Simon Baynes has lived and worked in Japan. His interests include Japanese, reading, writing and good television.

JOAN BROCKELSBY A Methodist lay preacher, Joan Brockelsby has published several books of poems. She takes part in readings and one of her longer poems on the theme of the crucifixion was featured in a BBC television broadcast.

GEORGE MACKAY BROWN lives in Orkney which (containing at its heart the Cathedral of Saint Magnus the Martyr) is the background to most of his work in verse and prose. The making of literature, he thinks, is craftsmanship first and foremost; the pyre has to be well and truly built for the flame of inspiration to fall.

ELIZABETH BURNS lives and works in Edinburgh where she is a member of Stramullion, a feminist publishing co-operative. Her poems are well received at readings, and *Saint Catherine's Monastery* won first prize in the Edinburgh City Poetry Competition, 1987.

CATHERINE BYRON Born 1947, grew up in Belfast, and went to Somerville College, Oxford. Her collection *Settlements* (1985) and the sequence *Samhain* (1987) are both published by Taxus Press. 'St Govnet, leaving Innisheer' is to be published in *Prospice*.

SANDY CONWAY was born in Leicestershire and now lives in Surrey. Married with three children, she works as a Southwark Pastoral Auxiliary in the parish of All Saints, Kenley.

STANLEY COOKE Born in Birmingham, 1926, left school at 14, worked as junior clerk, then took a drawing office apprenticeship. Started writing in his late teens and at the same time took up letter cutting in stone as a hobby. Lived in various parts of England as well as in Germany. for two years, returning eventually to Warwickshire where he now works as a lecturer in Further Education.

DENNIS R. CORBYN An ecumenical Christian, now retired from editorial and translation work but continuing to practise as a writer and artist. His work has been much influenced by periods of poverty, ill-health and mental conflict, also by wartime experiences, and a love of English writing, of animals and of the countryside.

SISTER JENNIFER DINES was born in 1938 and grew up in Brightlingsea, Essex. A member of a Roman Catholic religious order, The Congregation of Our Lady, she teaches Biblical Studies at Heythrop College in the University of London. Her poems have appeared in various magazines and anthologies, including *English, Outposts, The Month*.

BROTHER AIDAN DOHERTY was born in 1926 in Wexford, Ireland. He is a member of the teaching order of Christian Brothers and has worked in the North of England and West Africa. He holds degrees and diplomas from educational establishments in England, Ireland, France and the United States. He has written frequently on literary matters but his poetry, secular and religious, reflects the biblical lives of the people of Liberia and Sierra Leone, among whom he has taught since 1958. The poem *Joseph* is an extract from a choral piece performed in Yekeba, Liberia. Doherty's work has been published in several countries, most recently Peru.

SUE ELKINS, a Londoner living in Nottingham, is a freelance writer and broadcaster, involved in media liaison and adult education. She has had her poetry published in several magazines and books.

ALICE FAIRCLOUGH A native of Tyneside, orphaned and adopted in babyhood, she was educated at a convent school and Liverpool University. Thereafter she taught English Literature, her preference being the seventeeth-century Metaphysical poets. Now retired, she spends her time gardening, writing, painting in watercolour and translating Italian.

FATHER PETER FENWICK Born 1918 in Eastbourne, Sussex, he served in the Army 1939-46, and was mentioned in despatches 1940. Worked in the

Foreign Office and Ministry of Defence and was awarded an MBE in 1959. His wife died in 1968, leaving him with two young children. Joined the Roman Catholic religious order Institute of Charity in 1979. Ordained priest 1984, currently serving in Bexhill-on-Sea, Sussex. Began writing verse as POW in Germany. Published mostly in small poetry magazines. Enjoys sailing, swimming and walking.

EDITH FORREST is a retired teacher of English. She has written several short pieces of verse. *Thanksgiving* is her first published poem.

OLIVE FRASER studied English at Aberdeen University and at Cambridge where she won the Chancellor's Gold Medal for Poetry in 1935. Family illness and, later, the war interrupted her studies. She died in 1977 and in her own lifetime little of her work was published. Yet despite ill health, both mental and physical, she won two awards from the Scottish Arts Council for a play and for lyrics in Scots, one of which, *VE Day*, was published in *Lines Review*, following the posthumous collection of her work, *The Pure Account* (AUP, 1981), which was put together by Helena Shire. Olive Fraser brings to her later work a mastery of symbol and rhyme which harks back to the 'makars', the great poets of Scotland's past.

JOY FRENCH has been writing poetry since childhood. Her particular interest is in creating poems to be read aloud and linked with familiar texts of Scripture. Joy French became a Christian when she was thirty-nine and working in Uganda.

JAN GODFREY Born 1937 in Bromley, Kent, where she still lives. Married, with four grown-up children. Works as an infant teacher and freelance writer. Enjoys water colour painting and finds that writing poetry is often painting with words. 'fenscape', which was based on observation during a journey to Norfolk, won the Fellowship of Christian Writers Poetry Competition in 1987.

FRANCESCA GREEN is a singer living in Edinburgh who has an active interest in poetry, journalism and photography. Born in Yorkshire, she studied French and Italian at Newnham, Cambridge, and went on to complete her M.Litt on 'Gerard de Newall and Dante' at Edinburgh University. In May 1987 she exhibited with Women Live artists in Edinburgh. Her poems are published in magazines and she gives readings. She read her Chernobyl sequence at the Peace Festival, Edinburgh.

ALISTAIR HALDEN Educated at Glasgow University, he became an English teacher. A number of his poems have won prizes in poetry competitions, including the Greenwich Festival 1984 and the Scottish Open Competition in 1985. Other poems have appeared in magazines, including *Outposts*, *Chapman* and *Christian Poetry*.

MARTYN HALSALL was a schoolboy in Southport, Lancs, a teacher in Dorset, and a student in London, before he became a journalist. He worked on regional newspapers and joined *The Guardian* in 1980 as Churches Correspondent. Now Northern Industrial correspondent. He is married with two daughters and lives in Tottington, Lancs. His non-journalistic interests include gardening, walking, 1970s rock music, films and local politics.

JILL HARRIS lives in London, where she works as Assistant Editor with Scripture Union. Her own published material includes poems and fiction.

ROSEMARY HECTOR comes from Northern Ireland and now lives in Bath. The mother of three children, she is concerned with excellence in poetry and has won the Edinburgh City Poetry Prize.

NANCY HOPKINS was born in Virginia, Co. Cavan, Ireland. She has always been interested in writing. Before coming to London in 1955 she wrote several children's plays which were performed locally on stage. In 1958 she was seconded from the Civil Service to a posting in Germany for a three-year term. A member of the Society of Civil Service Authors and also of The Catholic Poetry Society, she has produced short stories and articles, as well as *Light and Shade* a collection of poetry published by the Civil Service Poetry Workshop.

SISTER MARGARET IRVING O.P. lives in Harare, Zimbabwe, where she teaches English literature. For many years she taught speech and drama, but now aged 82 has decided to 'slow down'. Her hobby is writing spiritual verse and she takes a full part in the life of her Order.

ALAN JACKSON After working his way through the free thinking of the sixties, Alan Jackson has come to a deep awareness of the centrality of the cross in human history and the life of the individual. Now 'a friend of the Christus', his works reflect the overriding importance of the spiritual dimension to life. He has published a number of books, including *The Heart of the Sun*, from which the poems included here have been taken.

SIMON JONES Born in Leicester 1956. Read history in Manchester and worked as a journalist for seven years, specializing in advertising, financial services and business travel. 'Moroccan Journey' arose from a trip to the opening of the Hyatt Regency Hotel in Casablanca. Simon is now training for the ministry and hopes to work in an inner city church.

THE REV. GRAHAM KINGS is Acting Principal of the St Andrew's Institute for Mission and Evangelism in the Diocese of Mount Kenya East. Graham Kings has seen his poems published in various magazines including Church Missionary Society magazines and *Christian*.

SISTER MARY LAURENCE SPB was born in 1937. In 1959 she joined an Anglican religious order whose chief work is intercessory prayer. She sent her poems to the anthology at the request of some of the sisters in her community.

K. LLOYD-THOMPSON's poem *The Breaking Heart of Simone Weil* is an exerpt from his 1987 Seatonian Prize-winning poem *The Grave Humours of Simone Weil*. Simone's 'proof' of God was the Presence of his Absence. K. Lloyd-Thompson's current work in quantum field theory appears to suggest that time only moves forward in the presence of its absence. To be infinitely full of time is then also to be timeless.

CHARLES LOVELL Born in London and lives in Rickmansworth, Herts. A retired Civil Servant who has contributed to Civil Service Poetry and other collections, including *100 Contemporary Christian Poets*, also published by Lion.

THE REV. TONY LUCAS is vicar of St Michael's Church, Stockwell, in South London. His poetry has appeared in a variety of magazines and anthologies in Britain and America.

RAYNE MACKINNON In spite of debilitating mental illness, Rayne Mackinnon has maintained an intellectual life of great integrity. His vocation is prayer and poetry. He was received into the Roman Catholic Church while he was a patient in a high security mental hospital and also became an associate of the Community of the Transfiguration, whose rule is based on simplicity and prayer. He has published four collections of verse, the last being *Northern Elegies* (Netherbow Arts Centre). His great mentor is St John of the Cross. Edwin Muir's poetry has been a 'fifth Gospel'. He enjoys listening to music, reads widely and studies Italian because of his love for Dante.

FRANK MORLEY Born in London in 1919, his working life was spent in a bank. He retired in 1978 and now has time to pursue his main interests: amateur dramatics, painting and woodworking and, particularly, writing poetry. His poems have appeared in *Christian Poetry*, produced by the Fellowship of Christian Writers.

WILLIAM NEILL Born 1922, this ex-airman, ex-teacher, now spends all his time trying to catch poetry in Galloway. He writes in three languages: Gaelic, Scots and English. 'Candles' is his translation from his own Gaelic. He was crowned Bard at the Inverness Mod in 1969 and has published eight collections of poetry. 'Sermon on Midlent Sunday', and 'Church History' appear in *Wild Places* (Luath Press, 1985). Other poems have appeared in magazines and his most recent collection of verse in the three languages of Scotland, *Making Tracks*, was published in 1988 by Gordon Stevenson.

FATHER KEVIN NICHOLS Born in 1929, he read English at Cambridge and became a priest, teacher and student chaplain. Now a parish priest in County Durham, he has written widely on literature and education.

M.J. NORMAN In spite of having been deaf since the age of six she was able to qualify as a school teacher. She taught until she became totally deaf after a car accident. 'God has used my love of poetry to comfort me and sustain my faith.'

HILARY OSCAR BRIAN O'NEIL Born in Liverpool and educated at Liverpool Institute and Sefton Park Teachers Training College, but now retired from teaching. Poems, mostly religious, have been published in many magazines. Author of hymns which have been widely used.

MICHEAL O'SIADHAIL Born in Dublin. He has published five collections of poetry, three in Irish, two in English – the latest being *Springnight* (Bluett, 1983) and *The Image Wheel* (Bluett, 1985). In 1982 he received the Irish American Cultural Institute's award for literature. At present on leave from a professorship at the Dublin Institute for Advanced Studies, he is a well-known linguistic scholar and a member of Aosdana (an elected body of distinguished Irish artists).

HAZEL PALMER began writing in 1982, mainly poetry. She is a language and Bible College graduate. Her interests include music and voluntary work at a speech therapy clinic. Born in Kent, she now lives in North Yorkshire.

EVANGELINE PATERSON was born in Limavady, County Londonderry, grew up in Dublin, and now lives in Leicester. She is married with three children. She edits *Other Poetry* magazine and is currently holder of an East Midland Arts writing bursary. Her poems have been published by Taxus Press and are widely anthologized.

NEIL PERRY Born in Chelmsford, Essex, where he still lives. Interests include gardening, reading, history, poetry and walking. He is currently unemployed.

CHRIS PORTEOUS is the solicitor to the Commissioner of Police at New Scotland Yard. He is married, with four daughters. Many of his hymns have been included in modern hymn books and his poems have been widely published in books and magazines.

DAVID PULLINGER had his first poem published in a school collection in 1968. Since then he has continued to write while earning a living as a mathematician, professional musician, archaeologist, factory workhand, gardener and computer consultant. He is currently Director of the Society, Religion and Technology Project for the Church of Scotland.

AMY PURDON was born in 1948. Widowed very recently, she is considering her future, which she hopes will include writing, music, walking, gardening, time for friends and family, reading and silence. She is a Companion to the Sisters of the Love of God (an Anglican contemplative community) and a member of the Friends of the Earth.

TESSA RANSFORD Director of the Scottish Poetry Library and founder/organizer of the School of Poets (1981). Tessa was born in India and educated in Scotland. Later she lived and worked in Pakistan for eight years. She has published five volumes of poetry, of which the latest are *Shadows from the Greater Hill* (Ramsay Head Press, Edinburgh) and *A Dancing Innocence* (Macdonald, Edinburgh).

MYRA REEVES Born 1909, she has been writing verse since childhood. Spent fifty fulfilled years as a wife and mother in Ludlow. Now living as a widow in Wrexham, she enrolled in the local Poetry Workshop in 1987, from which she has received much stimulation and encouragement.

JENNY ROBERTSON Always wanted to be a writer, but growing up in Glasgow, and the experience of working with displaced persons in Northern Germany, made her a social worker. Housebound because of family commitments she went back to writing. She has published novels for children and young people. A collection of poems, *Beyond the Border*, was published in 1988 (Chapman New Writing Series).

JOAN ROWBOTTOM Born in the city of Nottingham, she now lives in rural Nottinghamshire. She has been a member of the Nottingham Poetry Society and the International Fellowship of Christian Writers. She has broadcast her work and gives poetry readings.

GODFREY RUST works at Gallup Poll, managing the department which produces pop charts for Radio 1 and *Top of the Pops*, having ventured into the music business as a journalist after completing a Philosophy and Literature degree at Warwick University, where he won the *Birmingham Post* Universities' Poetry Prize. He stopped writing around 1975 when he found he had nothing to say, began again in 1980 as a direct consequence of a revitalized faith in God. Now married, he gives performances at concerts, writes songs, plays the guitar and runs marathons.

GEOFFREY SMITH currently works as Director of the Centre for Applied Christian Studies at Westhill College, Birmingham. He is an Anglican priest. He has been writing poems for a number of years and has published two collections, *Undoing Theology in Red Sneakers* and *Landscapes of the Heart* (Canon Books, Birmingham).

SISTER PAMELA STOTTER was born in Cheshire and later worked as a primary school teacher in Shrewsbury. Having gone to live in Ireland she joined a religious community, the Sisters of Mercy, and studied for a degree in theology and philosophy. She has had a number of hymn texts published and is involved in adult religious education in the diocese of Killaloe.

THE REV. TERENCE TOWERS is an Anglican priest, born in Norfolk and working in Durham, where he has been vicar of Ushaw Moor for over twenty years. His contacts with Orthodoxy date back to his student days. His wife is Orthodox and he has many friends in that Communion.

JEAN MACDONALD WATT Born 1915 in Reading of Scottish and Welsh parentage, she has lived in Scotland since 1933. She is a mother and grandmother, and was at one time a social worker. Her interests are music, painting and writing. Her published work includes *Paradox and Other Poems* (Macdonald, 1954) and prose translations from French and German. 'Stillpoint' was published in *The Tablet*.

GEORGE WESTON Born 1914, he left school at fourteen. During the war he worked for the War Agricultural Committee, driving a tractor plough. A poem written in these years disappeared in the bombing of London. A lay reader in the Church of England for twenty-eight years, and a church organist for thirty years George now describes himself as 'a good old has-been'.

DOREEN WHITTAM has six children and fifteen grandchildren. She has been a bank clerk, smallholding helper, freelance journalist and teacher. She and her husband, who are both retired, live in Essex with their youngest, Downs Syndrome, son.

MARGUERITE WOOD is a Suffolk poet, born in Ipswich. She has published four collections of poetry and a fifth is in preparation. Her poems have appeared in many magazines and anthologies and she is an assistant editor of *Envoi* poetry magazine. A physiotherapist, she has a history degree and enjoys contemporary music and painting.

VERONICA ZUNDEL is part-time Assistant Editor of *Third Way* magazine and a freelance writer and editor. She has compiled the *Lion Book of Famous Prayers* and the *Lion Book of Christian Classics*. Her columns from *Christian Woman* magazine, for which she won the Best Specialist Columnist award in the first Magazine Publishing Awards, are published by Monarch as *Life and other Problems*.

A selection of top titles from LION PUBLISHING

C.S. LEWIS William Griffin	£5.95 ☐
GEORGE MACDONALD William Raeper	£5.95 ☐
CLEMO: A LOVE STORY Sally Magnusson	£3.95 ☐
THE SHADOWED BED Jack Clemo	£3.95 ☐
LILITH George MacDonald	£2.50 ☐
PHANTASTES George MacDonald	£2.50 ☐
SONS AND BROTHERS Elizabeth Gibson	£2.99 ☐
TALIESIN Stephen Lawhead	£2.99 ☐
MERLIN Stephen Lawhead	£3.50 ☐
EMPYRION ONE Stephen Lawhead	£2.95 ☐
EMPYRION TWO Stephen Lawhead	£2.95 ☐
IN THE HALL OF THE DRAGON KING Stephen Lawhead	£2.99 ☐
THE WARLORDS OF NIN Stephen Lawhead	£2.99 ☐
THE SWORD AND THE FLAME Stephen Lawhead	£2.99 ☐

All Lion paperbacks are available from your local bookshop or newsagent, or can be ordered direct from the address below. Just tick the titles you want and fill in the form.

Name (Block letters) ....

Address ....

....

Write to Lion Publishing, Cash Sales Department, PO Box 11, Falmouth, Cornwall TR10 9EN, England.

Please enclose a cheque or postal order to the value of the cover price plus:

UK: 60p for the first book, 25p for the second book and 15p for each additional book ordered to a maximum charge of £1.90.

OVERSEAS: £1.25 for the first book, 75p for the second book plus 28p per copy for each additional book.

BFPO: 60p for the first book, 25p for the second book plus 15p per copy for the next seven books, thereafter 9p per book.

Lion Publishing reserves the right to show on covers and charge new retail prices which may differ from those previously advertised in the text or elsewhere, and to increase postal rates in accordance with the Post Office.